BETWEEN THE HILLS

The story of Lilley,
a Chiltern Village

Roy Pinnock

The Book Castle

For the purpose of accurate historical detail old currency rates have been used throughout this book.

Dedicated to Marion, my wife, typical of all the good people mentioned in the pages of this book.

First published July 1993
by
The Book Castle
12 Church Street
Dunstable
Bedfordshire
LU5 4RU

ISBN 1 871199 02 6

Typeset by Jefferson Typesetting, Maxet House, Luton.
Printed in Great Britain by The Alden Press, Oxford.

Acknowledgements

I am indebted to the many people who have chatted to me of their memories; who have welcomed me into their homes, and loaned documents, letters and photographs and interested themselves in this book. I am most grateful also to the Book Castle for republishing my three small books on village life in this one new volume.

Sources of information: The Vestry, St. Peter's Church, Lilley; the former Lilley School; Lilley Parish Council; Mr W. Branch Johnson, of Welwyn; the Sowerby family; Queries Editor, The Field Magazine; the Archivist, the Cumberland, Westmorland and City of Carlisle Record Office; the British Museum Newspaper Library; S.R. Meager for the Hertfordshire dialect; Mrs R.J. Lowe of Flitwick; Canon the Rev. Howard Senar; the late Mr G.L. Evans of Pirton; Hertfordshire Countryside; Tattersalls of London; Hertfordshire County Archivist; Bedford County Archivist; Lilley Rectory — 1868-1904 by Edmund Haviland, 1963; Canon Francis Aidan Hibbert's The Story of a Small Village; Fifty Years Ago, by Walter Rose; Southgate's A Textbook of Modern English History; Curator of Hitchin Museum, who gave permission to use the Lilley File compiled by the late Reginald Hine; Mr. Edmund Holmes who loaned the accounts of village blacksmith Edward Cain, and a book called Little Jack of All Trades; the Vicar, Churchwardens and Parochial Church Council of St. Mary Magdalene's Church, Offley, who gave permission to use old parish magazines; and the Curator, Luton Museum and Art Gallery, who gave permission to quote from Luton and the Hat Industry, by Charles Freeman. And last, but not least, my hearfelt thanks to Julie Jefferson for preparing the manuscript for this book.

— B.R. Pinnock, Lilley, Herts, February, 1993

About the Author

Roy Pinnock was closely involved in all aspects of life in Lilley during the 48 years he lived there. He is now a Church of England Reader who works with those recovering from mental illness and stress. He presently lives with his wife Marion, born and bred in Lilley, at Barton-le-Clay near Luton. They have three children and eight grandchildren.

St. Peter's Church, Lilley, drawn by Heather Whatling, eldest of the author's three grand-daughters.

Photographs and Sketches

Those who loaned original photographs are identified in the captions thus:

PC - Phyllis Chapman

MC - Michael Cooper

DG - David Greenhough

RM - Robin MacKonochie

BO - Betty Offer

BT - Brian Taylor

MT - Michael Toyer

JT - Joy Trimnell

Those photographs not identified as above belong to the Author.

❖ ❖ ❖ ❖ ❖

The author would like to thank the above for their willingness to loan photographs. He would also like to thank his grand-daughter, Heather Whatling, for the sketch of Lilley Church; Brian Taylor and Chris Jackson for the map of Lilley village; David Greenhough, for the book jacket and the area map; Ted Holmes, for the original small sketches and Shirley Ogden, of Barton-le-Clay, for typing out 'odds and ends'.

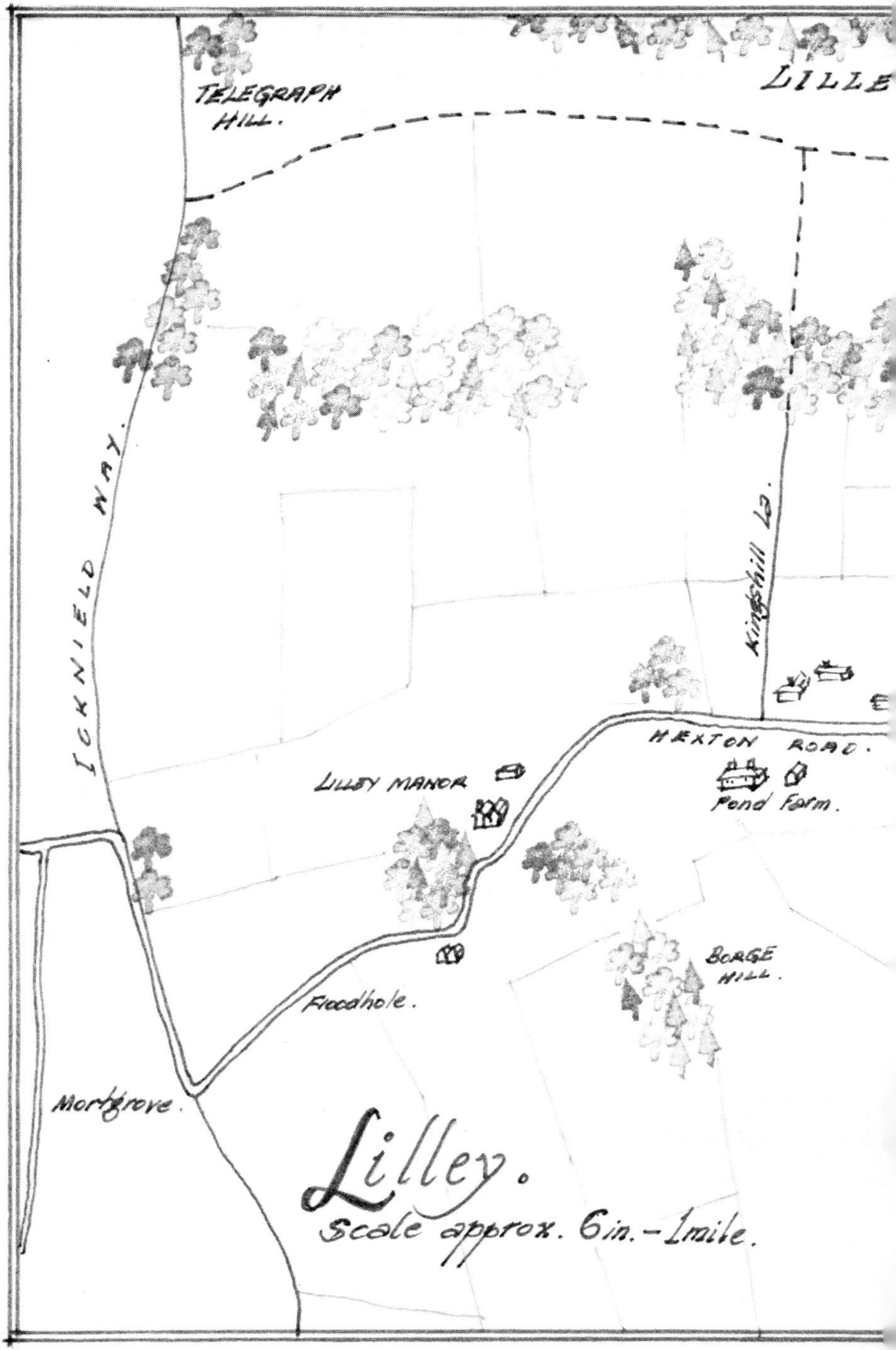
TELEGRAPH HILL.
LILLE
ICKNIELD WAY.
Kingshill La.
HEXTON ROAD.
LILLEY MANOR
Pond Farm.
BORGE HILL.
Floodhole.
Morthgrove.
Lilley.
Scale approx. 6in.-1mile.

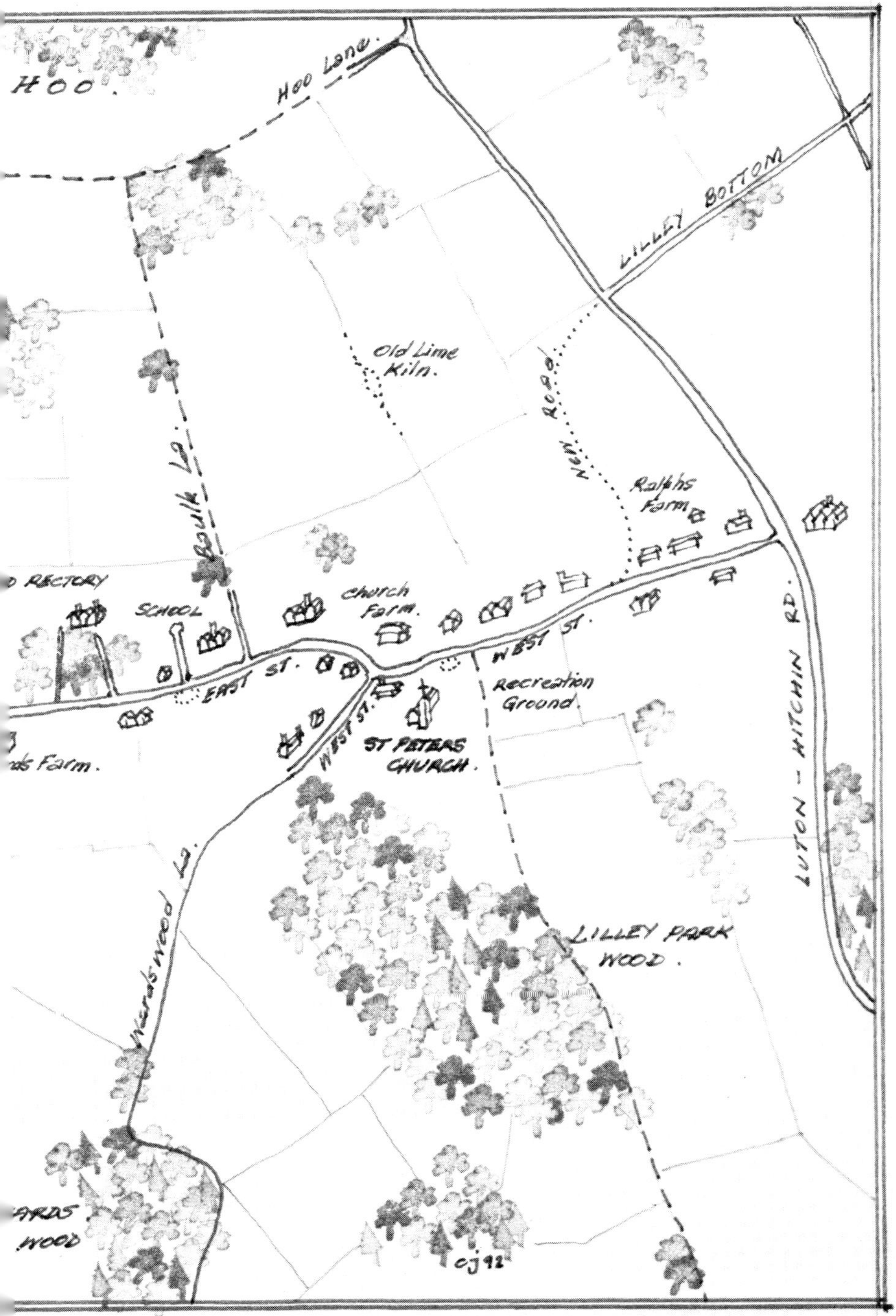
HOO.
Hoo Lane.
LILLEY BOTTOM
Old Lime Kiln.
New Road
Ralphs Farm
RECTORY
SCHOOL
Baulk La.
Church Farm.
EAST ST.
WEST ST.
WEST ST.
Recreation Ground
ST PETERS CHURCH.
Farm.
LUTON - HITCHIN RD.
LILLEY PARK WOOD.
Wards Wood La.
WOOD
CJ 92

THE LILLEY ARMS

Contents

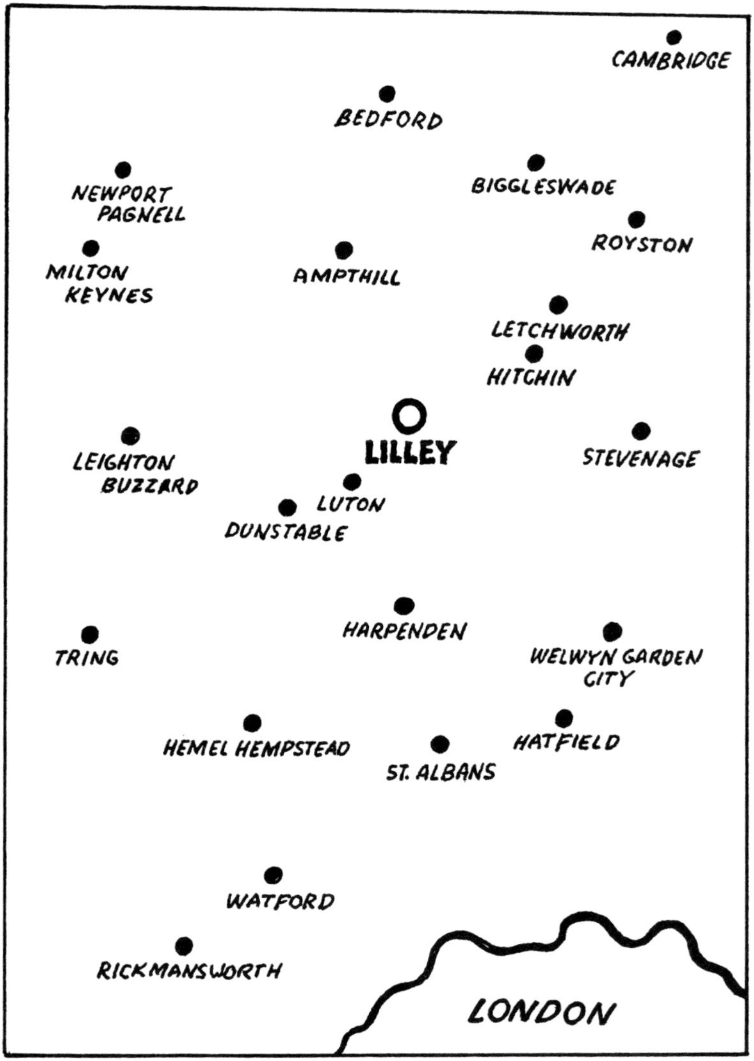
CAMBRIDGE
BEDFORD
NEWPORT PAGNELL
BIGGLESWADE
ROYSTON
MILTON KEYNES
AMPTHILL
LETCHWORTH
HITCHIN
LILLEY
LEIGHTON BUZZARD
STEVENAGE
LUTON
DUNSTABLE
HARPENDEN
TRING
WELWYN GARDEN CITY
HEMEL HEMPSTEAD
HATFIELD
ST. ALBANS
WATFORD
RICKMANSWORTH
LONDON

Chapter 1

Viewed Through The Vestry

LILLEY. Lying roughly five miles from Hitchin and next-door to Luton, "our village" is just in the county of Hertford: indeed, its southern-most boundary is also the county boundary; a small village of five hundred-odd souls cocking a snook, as it were, at the huge town of Luton, as if to say, "Swallow us if you can".

The village, long and straggling, each side of a single street, nestles amid the Chiltern Hills, a geographical position it occupied long before William came from Normandy to conquer we English. It boasts a church and two public houses. There used to be a post office and a school, both now closed. Its interests and ambitions are jealously guarded and promoted by a seven-strong parish council, and quite recently a Lilley Society. An annual fete gives its inhabitants the chance of a frolic on the recreation ground; its pheasants afford a deal of pleasure in their demise to the dinner table. Several attempts have been made to organise a youth club, but all have inevitably failed — the young ones of Lilley do not, perhaps, like being organised; its menfolk mostly work in surrounding townships and, with their ladies, tend their gardens with loving care. In short, it is a village like any other village.

The purpose of this book is to try to recapture life as it used to be lived before the transition to a commuters' paradise was made; a way of life that all too soon will lie buried with those who lived it. In this attempt I have interviewed countless people who have reached the "autumn" of their lives, alas many have since died. I have also searched diligently those records still available — documents, registers, personal letters where I have found that the names recorded take on new life; they materialise from the musty vellum into people who trod the same paths as we today. Who cultivated the same gardens, who tilled the same fields; who loved and married, and raised a family. Names like William Deacon, John Foster, William Cain, Thomas Conisbee, John Field, Thomas Irons, James Irons, Daniel Gutteridge, William Conisbee, John Bates.

Our first glimpse into the past is taken from the Churchwardens' Account Book, which starts on May 13, 1802. The Wardens' income then was derived from a church rate levied annually by a vestry meeting.

Some entries chosen at random: 1802, the bellringers were paid 2s. for each session; Richard Lane was paid £19 10s. for repairing the steeple and the top of the church; beer for the workmen when repairing the church cost £3 11s. 8d. — quite a few gallons compared with today's prices; J. Smith was paid 2s. for supplying "ye bread for Communion". In 1803 Ed. Gray received 3s. 6d. for bringing materials from Offley; a carpenter received 10s. for repairing the stocks, which were located outside the church gate; and then follows an entry repeated many times in the following years: "Pd. for catching 43½ doz. sparrows for two years, 7s. 3d". Why on earth the Churchwardens paid out money for sparrows beats me. I've heard tell of "sparrow pie". Perhaps the Wardens bought them for this purpose?

We can begin now to get a picture of local tradesmen: Richard Lane was employed on the steeple of the church, which, being a Hertfordshire "spike", was leaded — a builder, perhaps. John Smith kept a shop, for he supplied "ye bread for Communion". Ed. Gray was a carrier. A man called Newton, in 1804, was paid £1 17s. for plumbers' work on the church. Wm. Cain was the village blacksmith, and in 1804 received 4s. 3d. for ironwork to the stockhouse. Woodward was a shopkeeper, for, in addition to John Smith, he supplied bread for Communion. Dan Gutteridge supplied bricks, tiles and lime for £7 5s. 6d. John Field was a bricklayer and John Main another carrier, both being members of the Vestry. In 1808, the Wardens paid out 9s 7d. for 57½ dozen sparrows caught over a period of two months. It is a pity the accounts do not mention to whom the money was paid. We would then know the name of this industrious sparrow-catcher.

In 1810 we come across two more tradesmen. Dan Field whitewashed the church for £1 4s., and Henry Emmins received 4s. for firing when repairing the "top of the church".

Now let us jump ten years and see what we find. 1820: Wm. Pates was the Churchwarden disbursing the accounts. John Bates was licensee of the Red Lion, and William Conisbee of the Sugar Loaf. Posting a letter cost 2d. In 1810 two letters cost a shilling. The sparrow business had boomed. In the year 1820, 276 dozen of the poor creatures were purchased, but the price had increased to about 3½d. a dozen.

A decade further on George Atkins was paid 5s. for three bushels of coal. Thomas Barrett was a bricklayer and William Clark a painter and carpenter. William Pates supplied bread and wine for Communion and received money for sparrows — a clue at last to the identity of a sparrow-catcher, but it is not clear whether this one had caught them or was being reimbursed for paying someone else.

A directory, published some time after 1842, states: "Lilley or Lindley is a village and parish on the borders of Bedfordshire, five miles west of Hitchin Station and north-east of Luton, in the Hundred and Union of Hitchin and Pirton. The church is dedicated to St. Peter and the living is a rectory in the gift of St. John's College, Cambridge; the incumbent is the Rev. Miles Bland, DD. The area of the parish is 1,620 acres; and the population in 1841 was 475. The assessment to Income Tax was in 1842 £2,527. At Putteridge Bury, half a mile south, is a park. Mangrove Green and Cockernhoe Green are one and a half miles south." Then follows a list of tradesmen;

"Atkins and Clarke, wheelwrights; John Atwood, shoemaker; James Cain, boot and shoemaker; John Cain, blacksmith; Thomas Cain, dealer in plait; William Cain, blacksmith; Isaac Ebbs, grocer; William Ewer, farmer; William Ewer, junior, farmer; William Godfrey, grocer; William Gutteridge, farmer; Mrs. Dinah Hare, licensee the Red Lion; William Irons, farmer; Daniel Kentish, grocer; James Pates, licensee the Sowerby Arms (alias the Sugar Loaf), and John Taylor, farmer."

To return to the Wardens' Accounts. In 1845 we find William Cain as Churchwarden. Sparrows seem to have disappeared from the scene, and it becomes difficult to make out people's occupations, names only being mentioned; "To paid Ebbs, 2s." The writings of William Cain, however, are rather amusing. For instance: "To pavings and cartedg and puting down in the hile" (aisle). "To washing the surples." "To washing two surpellsess." "To mending a bell roap." "To cutting the thisels and netels." On December 25, he records: "To giting the holey and seting it."

A few more names come to light in 1846. Thomas Cain was paid 10s. for carting and gravel. Others receiving money were James Pates, Sarah Bradbury and Joseph Stevens. This same year Daniel Kentish took over as Churchwarden. On November 18, 1852, 1s. was paid for "Tolling a Knell for the Duke of Wellington". Members of the Vestry this year were Thomas Cain, James Pates, James Irons, William Cain and Daniel Kentish. In 1854 a new face was seen in the

Rev. W.R.P. Boggis, Curate.

In the six years, 1854 to 1860, that the Rev. Boggis was in the village he conducted twenty-seven wedding ceremonies, and of these twenty-five couples were "both of this parish". The Baptism Register reveals that in one six-year period 138 children were baptised, an average of almost two a month! The occupations of the fathers ranged from seventy-seven labourers, four farmers, six gamekeepers, to one plait dealer and one carman. A study of genealogy would reveal that many village families are inter-related and could trace back their association with each other well over a hundred and fifty years just by examining church records. The Toyers, for instance, can be traced back five generations by examining one register; they are associated with the Penns and Humphries.

A Church Rate Book for 1862 serves just now to throw a little more light on to our picture of the past. In it we find that Thomas Sowerby was Lord of the Manor, and that of the 113 rateable properties, only thirty-four actually paid the church rate . . . to the tune of £19 for this particular year.

Thomas Sowerby owned sixty-seven of the 113 properties above, George Atkins thirteen (he paid a rate on an orchard, two roods in extent, as well as on his other property), William Ewer six (including a house and land of ten acres), George Irons seven (land at Lilley Bottom), Lady Salusbury four (forty-one acres near Lilley Hoo, five acres at Little Offley, one acre at Oakleys, and thirty-eight at Offley Vicarage), Richard Marsh two (land and a plantation at Little Offley, six acres in extent), and the Rev. Wills (seventeen acres at Lilley Bottom).

Charles Cannon was the licensee of an inn at Mangrove, and also owned there two houses with gardens and a cottage; John Bates owned four properties, and Mrs. William Foster four, also at Mangrove.

The rate book records that in the parish, covering Lilley, Mangrove and parts of Offley, there were eight farms, four inns, but only two shops (one can only assume that more were opened at a later date). Some of the householders were: Widow Burton, James Bean, Thomas Brown, Edward Bodsworth, John Webb, Samuel Crane, James Davis, Charles Titmuss, Henry Humphrey, Hannah Dimmock, James Cherry, junior and senior, Samuel Goodge, Levi Marlow, Widow Humphries, Sarah Bradbury, Levi Bean, Edward Cain, Thomas Bland, George Wilson, William Clark and William Cain.

In the Wardens' Account Book, three more names appear in 1868: the Rev. A.C. Haviland, Roger Irons and John Attwood.

At Easter, 1870, the old church was used for the last time. I have often wondered where services were held in the interim before the present church was opened. A clue appears in entries for 1870. On September 9, someone was paid 4s. for "two days' work making and fixing candlesticks for the Tabernacle"; the accounts were approved at a vestry meeting held in "the temporary church" and on January 7, 1871, 8d. was paid for a "scraper at Tabernacle door". I have been informed that the temporary building was located in a meadow called Rueley Dell; was made of tin, and was used for about fourteen months.

Chapter 2

The Norman Church

It seems a pity that the old St. Peter's had to be demolished. What a treasure we should have had today! But from available evidence, and that is precious little, it would seem that the church was in a shocking condition.

As far as we know it was built around the middle of the twelfth century. This much is gathered from the remains of the chancel arch, which dates from about 1150, and is preserved as the organ chamber arch in the present building.

It is not known for certain who built the church. Prior to the Battle of Hastings, the owner of Lilley was a woman called Leveva, who was eventually evicted in favour of Ilbert de Lacy by William the Conqueror. Ilbert did not last long, however, for in 1086 Lilley was an independent Manor (it had previously been joined to Wellbury) belonging to Geoffrey de Beck. Then follows a blank of 100 years in Lilley's history, during which time a stone church was built on the edge of the Lord of the Manor's demesne. Who built the church? Well, it is probable that a family called Malet were responsible for the building, financially, at least.

After Geoffrey de Beck, the next owner who is recorded is William Malet whose ancestors had come over to England with William the Conqueror (and had founded a great family, with many estates all over the land, given as rewards for help in the Conquest), and eventually obtained Lilley. So it is possible we have them to thank for the old St. Peter's, although there is no direct evidence that we have.

By about 1450 Lilley was owned by a new type of landlord, one who bought estates for investment purposes and let out his land to farmers. Landowning had become very profitable by now, and it has been calculated that by the enclosing of land its value was doubled. It was at this point in history that much church restoration and beautifying was undertaken, no doubt because of the new-found wealth of landowners and wool merchants, many of whom made fortunes.

The twelfth-century St. Peter's Church, Lilley, demolished in 1871 to make room for the present church. Note the Hertfordshire 'spike' and the chimney from the fire that warmed the 'Squire's Pew'. BT

Several legacies were left to the old church, but these disappeared during the Reformation. The old windows, which had been small and narrow, were replaced by larger ones with the fashionable Perpendicular tracery, and were filled with coloured glass. The chancel was lengthened and a large window added, which was filled with stained glass rather later by Sir Nicholas Vaux, an owner of Lilley. It was a picture of Christ's crucifixion, with the inscription at the bottom: "Pray for the souls of Nicholas Vaux and Elizabeth his wife, who had this window made." The roof was rebuilt and the new flat one was decorated with carvings of angels and coloured shields of arms. At the west end was a small square belfry of wood surmounted by a leaded Hertfordshire "spike". A vestry was also added.

In 1552 the church possessed two chalices, four vestments of silk and velvet — white, red and green — and two copes of green silk. There were then four bells in the steeple and two handbells in the church. Before the altar a sanctuary lamp always burnt, its cost being met by an endowment consisting of the rent of three acres of arable land. The income from these was 1s. 6d. a year. The largest bell was recast in 1703, with the inscription: "George Chandler made me, 1703", and there is a record of the ancient Rogationtide procession in 1711. In the churchyard a new post for the sundial was made in 1706, and in 1713 John Butterfield, junior, was paid 6s. 11d. for setting up a pole at the rejoicings of the Peace of Utrecht.

In 1823, by all accounts, the church was in a sorry state. The pillaging of the Reformation and the twenty years of Puritan rule, when it is possible that only few services were held at Lilley, had just about finished off the fabric. In an attempt to improve things new benches, hat-pegs, kneelers and matting were provided. A new surplice was bought for two guineas; psalm singers were instituted and were paid 5s. a year: the gallery was repaired and the clarinet mended. A new bell was hung bearing the inscription: "T. Mears of London fecit 1827." The beautiful old glass was still in the windows, but in a bad state. Much glazing was done in 1824, and it was probably then that the fifteenth century glass disappeared.

We have to wait another forty-four years for a really authoritative description of the old St. Peter's. The writer was one Matthew Feakes:

"It was early in the year of 1868 that I first saw this church; it was then in a very dilapidated condition. It consisted of nave, chancel and small wooden tower, in which hung three bells (dated 1580, 1703 and 1827 — author). The entrance to the nave was through a low porch on the south side; the floor was the same level throughout nave and chancel. At the west end of the nave was a curious structure, which formed a gallery with open-slatted front, and from the upright timbers were cross-beams to which the bells were hung under the wooden tower; the bells were rung from this gallery floor. On the south side of the nave was the singers' gallery, which was a more modern structure with two rows of seats, and would seat about thirty people. At the date which I have mentioned the violin and bass viol had just been superseded by a harmonium; the player was a young man from the village, engaged at a salary of £1 per annum , using his own instrument, which he carried in every Sunday for the service.

"The roof of the nave had, I should imagine, been very fine in its day, with dark oak beams and cross-beams; the three principal cross beams had at each end the figure of an angel with wings partly spread; I may add these figures lacked various parts from decay. The pulpit, a lofty one, stood on the north side of the chancel arch, with prayer desk in front, each with panelled doors; overhead was suspended a large sounding-board; opposite, on the south side, was the squire's pew, a large square box with curtains and an open fireplace. The other pews were much the same, only smaller, some with doors and some without.

"On the south wall was the Houghton Tablet with the Latin inscription and dates 1636 and 1672. The centre aisle was covered with rush matting, hiding from view a very uneven floor, made of stones, bricks and tiles of many shapes and sizes. The nave contained four windows, one large and one small on either side; the large one on the north side had a few pieces of stained glass at the top, one piece being the Hertfordshire Stag.

"There was a small entrance door to the chancel on the south side; on the north wall of the chancel was the Docwra Monument, and a door led into the vestry, which had no outer door; on the floor of the chancel was a slab stone over the place where Sir George Warburton was buried in 1743, and one similar over Sir Benjamin Rawling, buried in 1775. The communion rail enclosed a small raised space under the east window; on one side of this window was the Ten Commandments, on the other side the Creed and Lord's Prayer. Such was Lilley Old Church in 1868."

Located outside the church gates were the village stocks, and if the Churchwardens' Accounts are anything to go by, as dilapidated as the church itself. The Rev. Miles Bland, DD, Rector of Lilley from 1823 to 1868, was a Justice of the Peace, and it was quite a common sight for the village constable to be waiting for him after morning service with some unfortunate to be summary committed to the stocks.

The clergy at this time were often country gentlemen, and mixed socially with landowners of their neighbourhood: they hunted, dined, entertained, farmed, and kept a large staff of servants. Many of them held rather a patronising view of their flock; rather than serving they were served. Miles Bland was not numbered among this class, however.

Succeeding Miles Bland was Arthur Coles Haviland. He was born in Cambridge. Educated at Eton and Cambridge, he married Jane Mary Knyvett, born at Windsor Castle, the daughter of a minor canon of Windsor, and took up his living at Lilley in the latter part of 1868. His family, who like their father and mother, were much beloved by village people, were Dora, Edmund and Eleanor, Reginald, Katharine, Joan, Wilfred, Margaret, Leonard, Aimee and Phyllis.

After Mr. Haviland became Rector he was inspired with an enthusiasm that enabled him to accomplish a task many would have shirked. He sought the eminent architectural advice of Mr. Thomas Jeykyll, of London, regarding the church, and decided then that the best plan was to rebuild. He raised several large donations (apart from his own) from parishioners towards a cost of just over £3,000 for a new building. The old church was used for the last time on Easter Day, 1870.

St. Peter's Church from the North and next to it Church Cottage. Roadman George Bishop used to live in another part of this cottage that has since been demolished. BO

The foundation stone of the new church of St. Peter was laid by Mrs. George Sowerby, and that of the Sowerby Chapel by her daughter Annie (Mrs. Fellowes) on St. Peter's Day (June 29), 1870. The vestry, chancel and nave were completed fourteen months afterwards, the tower being added at a later date.

The church throughout is faced with local undressed flint stones. The chancel is thirty-two feet long, sixteen feet wide, and the nave fifty-three feet long, twenty-five feet wide. The architecture is Early Decorated, though the lancet windows in the nave, which are exact copies of those in the old church, belong to an earlier period. The nave roof is completely timbered. The chancel roof is covered with coloured shields depicting various symbols of St. Peter.

Over the altar is a white marble cross. This has particular interest because, when the church was built, an altar cross was frowned upon in a church. Mr. Havilland determined not only to have one, but emphasised his view on the question by providing a large cross that almost dwarfed the altar. To prevent its removal he had it built into the wall.

The pulpit is made of oak from the old chapel of St. John's College, Cambridge (of which college Mr. Haviland was a Fellow) and which in 1871 was being pulled down.

Over the west door hangs the Sowerby hatchment, a copy of the family armorial bearings, placed temporarily on the outside of a family house or tomb upon the death of a member of the family, a custom, of course, no longer practised. Beneath the coat-of-arms is

The chancel of the second St. Peter's Church, candle-lit for a carol service. The Norman chancel arch from the first St. Peter's can be seen on the left as the organ arch.

the single word "Resurgam", meaning "I will rise again". The Sowerby Chapel commemorates various members of the family.

Above the tower is a weather vane erected to the memory of Richard James Bland, verger, sidesman, church councillor, Sunday School teacher and bellringer. Mrs. Susan Bland is also commemorated. She was appointed verger in 1909 at a salary of £1 6s. per annum.

Others whose memory is perpetuated within the hallowed

All dressed up and ready to go. Members of St. Peter's Church with the then Rector, the Rev. Aidan Hibbert, scholar and historical author. The author's great-grandmother, Susan Bland, is second from the right, middle row. BO

walls of St. Peter's are members of the Docwra family, particularly Thomas Docwra, senior, and Thomas his son. The former lived to be 84, and when Thomas, junior, died in 1620, a monument was built to them. It is now placed in the church porch. The elder was "reverenced for his gravity, wisdom, piety, justice and hospitality", and the younger was "worthily esteemed for his wisdom, judgments, moderation and liberal housekeeping". Below the monument is a very attractive little verse:

A Prevention of Forgetfulness.
This is the tomb of him who gave content.
By shunning that to which the world are bent.
He did not stoop to vain ambition's lure,
But deem'd his own more happy and more sure.
And this my due and last farewell I take,
Bound to protect His State and Children for His sake.

Also in the church porch are tablets to William Wade, BD, Rector of the village from 1798 to 1823, and to Daniel Houghton, son of Daniel Houghton, of Cheddington, Bucks, and Frances Carter, of Lilley, who died in 1672. In the porch floor are tablets to Sir George and Lady Warburton, and to Sir Benjamin Rawling, Lord of Lilley Manor during the infamous Enclosure of Land. Just inside the church, beneath the magnificent west window is the Baptistry, furnished to the memory of Ethel Naomi Allingham, a tireless worker for church and village and a Churchwarden for many years, who died in 1950, at the age of 71; also of her husband Frank Allingham, farmer, of Dog Kennel Farm, who died in 1947, aged 78: and of their daughter, Joan, who died at the age of 23, in 1931.

A huge picture of St. Christopher on the south wall is to the memory of Esther Cundall, governess of the village school for thirty-five years. Also on the south wall is a tablet to Louise Prouse Young, like Mrs. Allingham, a great social worker. Her husband, the late Arthur Young, was a Churchwarden for many years, and also at one time an overseer of the parish. The lych gate was built to the memory of Rector Haviland, who died in 1904.

There is only a small choir now, but before the First World War there were two rows of men and two rows of boys, under the watchful eye of Matthew Feakes, who thought nothing of clouting a boy over the head if he misbehaved! Matthew was quite a character.

A group of servants employed by the benevolent Lilley Rector, the Rev. Arthur Coles Haviland. The picture was taken in the grounds of the Rectory.   PC

He was a gardener by profession and years earlier had been responsible for laying out the grounds of the new Rectory, which Rector Haviland had built for his large family. Matthew was also a Churchwarden and a Parish Councillor, and also organised Lilley Clothing Club, in which village people saved money to withdraw at a later date and spend in Luton to clothe their offspring. On these occasions the village school was closed for half a day, everybody piling into the available village wagons, including "The Lilley Bus", poste haste for town.

Matthew Feakes is also remembered for his talking parrot. Its favourite expression was "Tell Feakes, tell Feakes". No doubt with a larger vocabulary, it could have told Feakes a lot, particularly about the village boys "scrumping" his apples!

A view of the present St. Peter's Church taken from the south-west corner of the churchyard. DG ▶

A view of Lilley's cricket ground taken from the church tower. The five gravestones beneath the tree commemorate members of the Cassel family. RM ▼

The Lilley Bus, loaded up and ready to start its daily journey to Luton, where it stopped at the old Horse and Jockey public house. BC

Chapter 3

Transport

About the middle of the Nineteenth Century an Act of Parliament restricted to four miles an hour all mechanically propelled machines on the open road and thus furthered the development of the traction engine. With these locomotives, slow and cumbersome, but capable of dealing with the heaviest loads, quite a number of long-distance hauls were made over Hertfordshire highways by the already well-established firm of Pickfords.

In the late nineteenth century the traction engine was applied to the tasks of threshing and ploughing. Now from the Hertfordshire fields came the whine of the threshing machine and rhythmic throb of the engine as more corn was fed into the drum. For ploughing operations, larger locomotives were used, as a winding drum had to be accommodated beneath the boiler. With one positioned on either side of the field the plough was hauled to and fro on the cable, the engines moving forward as necessary.

When travelling between farms on the narrow Victorian roads they took up most of the available width and, with escaping steam often frightened passing horses, the drivers were frequently reviled by those gentlemen out for a drive who had the misfortune to encounter them.

With the repeal of the above Act in 1896, steam lorries were soon to be seen on Hertfordshire roads. Steel-tyred wheels, no protection for the driver and stoker, they did good work and dealt with fairly heavy loads. Within a few years there was quite a variety passing along our highways — vertical boilers, horizontal boilers, overtypes and undertypes, and all now with some semblance of a driving cab. Other improvements followed and their number increased. Nightly the procession of Fodens, Manns, Robeys, Sentinels and others made their way out of London and through Hertfordshire to the Midlands and the North.

Despite these advances, however, as far as Lilley was concerned the horse was to remain supreme for a decade or more

The history of this car cannot be traced. Did it belong to the Sowerby family? No doubt, it was seen many times in Lilley. PC

yet; although a few motor cars did appear on the local scene. I am told that the first one in the village was owned by Thomas George Sowerby. One can imagine the interest shown by village men when the squire decided to take his family out for a spin. What these worthies would say if they could see the number of the "bloody noisy things" that tear through our beautiful countryside today I imagine would make interesting but unprintable reading!

To return to the horse, of interest fifty or sixty years ago was the weekly visit to Trussell's bakery of a huge miller's dray drawn by three magnificent Shires. It must have been quite a sight to watch these splendid beasts feeding from their nosebags; flinging up their heads and spilling a few grains of oats, hungrily devoured by sparrows, who fought, fluttered and chirped about the horses' feet.

It was a sad day, I think, when fine animals like these disappeared from the rural scene. Their strength, their patience, their friendliness surely being typical of a way of life that would seem to be of far more benefit than today's rush and tear.

When historians come to write our story, with what will they typify us? Motor cars, jets, computers, word processors? All man-made machines, not possessing the breath of life bestowed only by the Almighty.

The railways used horses similar to those used by the miller delivering to Trussell's. The railway drays had heavy horses with

HARNESS

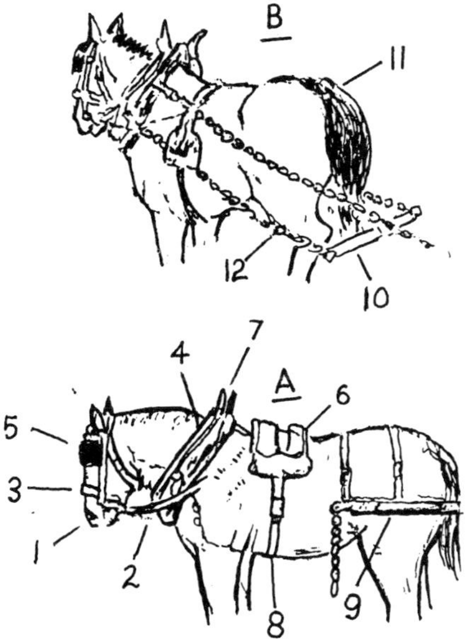

1 BIT
2 REINS
3 BRIDLE
4 COLLAR
5 BLINKERS
6 SADDLE
7 HAMES
8 GIRTH
9 BREECHING
10 SWINGLE TREE
11 CRUPPER
12 TRACE
A CART GEAR
B PLOUGH GEAR

STABLE LANTERN

great hooves feathered with masses of hair which was combed out and flowing, and the manes were thick and long, sometimes plaited.

The railways were rich and could afford the best for their animals, often employing men solely for the purpose of buying hay.

Trappings for horses were also many and varied, the colours of the head-bands, the variety of the horse-brasses, the decorated whips with ribbons and copper bands, the bells and various ornaments making in themselves an interesting study.

At one time Lilley boasted four carriers: Jabez Cain, Harry Trussell, Harry Taylor and Jim Cherry, each making the trip to Luton on different weekdays. Harry Taylor's wagon had a canvas top and held twelve people. Jabez Cain owned a carriage called a "fly" which was often used for weddings.

If one really wanted to travel in style, however, one would use the "Lilley Bus", which ran from the Lilley Arms and the Red Lion to Luton and Hitchin three times a week. The horses, stabled at the former inn, were groomed by "Topper" Cain (so-called, perhaps, because of the head-gear he sported while driving the "Lilley Bus"), Pete Taylor and Bob Titmuss. The "bus" was owned by Jabez Cain, who seemed to have had his fingers in a great many pies!

When Maud Holmes (Harry Taylor's daughter) was a girl, the annual Sunday School treat was an occasion of anticipation, opportunities of going beyond Luton or Hitchin being very rare. Maud can remember travelling on such outings in a charabanc, but how was the journey undertaken before the age of steam or the internal combustion engine? In all probability the party would travel in a wagon and two horses. I have a mental picture of a wagon that was used at Church Farm when I was a boy. It was higher at the front and back than in the middle, had two large wheels at the back and two smaller ones at the front. This could have been the type used for village outings, but no one has been able to verify this for me. The wagon at Church Farm was painted blue with red wheels.

The village going to church must have been quite a sight. The old ladies from the almshouses walked in their bonnets and unmistakeable red shawls. Putteridge Bury staff drove from the Park in a brake drawn by two horses. Mr. Farr and family, from Mangrove Hall Farm, arrived in a very low horse-drawn vehicle more like a buggy, his sons riding horseback. Mr. Bailey, from Mortgrove, and the Allinghams also drove to church. The horses were stabled at the Lilley Arms for the duration of the service. The most common form of transport, of course, to church or anywhere else for that matter, was by walking. Many of today's unused footpaths were, fifty, sixty or more years ago, very important short cuts. The path from the church across to Beech Hill, and the one from the same spot to the top of Hollybush Hill being the two bearing the heaviest foot traffic.

If you were a child in a well-to-do family after the turn of the century you might possibly be lucky enough to possess a goat carriage or a donkey and trap. The goat would be harnessed in the same way as the donkey, but the carriage would be much smaller. As

A village celebration in the 1930s, complete with old farm waggons; the 'Brownie' in the foreground is Phyllis Chapman, still living in Lilley. PC

far as I know, no one in Lilley possessed such a carriage.

The first mechanical buses, with open top decks, started plying along the A505 about 1916, although this is not verified. There were then three a day. When negotiating the hitherto notorious Beech Hill just outside the village, the conductor always had a block of wood to hand, ready to drop behind a wheel when the vehicle invariably stopped halfway up the hill. All the passengers were expected to disembark and give a push. Which made travelling in the "Lilley Bus" much more relaxing . . . for the passengers, at least!

The late Charles Bland claimed the distinction of being the first person in the village to have owned motorised transport.

Charles Bland and his sister Lilian on an early motorcycle in the garden still in existence in East Street, Lilley.

This early model of a sporting car belonged to Charles Bland an uncle of the author.

He once recalled that one morning he was starting into life the engine of his Triumph motor-cycle when Harry Cain, a steam engine driver, sauntered up, thumbs in his trouser pockets, and enquired how Charles "got steam up". When told that he hadn't to do this, he replied: "Well, that's a bloody rum go" or words to that effect, and off he went, scratching his head in amazement.

Chapter 4

Background

The aforementioned Harry Cain, like many other village men, almost certainly wore really thick, serviceable trousers, a waistcoat and probably a shirt without a collar. All would sport either side whiskers or a moustache. Everyday clothes for the womenfolk were a course, serviceable dress, a stout calico apron and a shawl.

Two or three decades earlier that quaint, picturesque and most convenient of garments, a smock, would very likely be seen around the village. In Hertfordshire, they were often worn by the agricultural worker, being very warm and comfortable and, of course, the carrier is nearly always depicted wearing a smock; a jovial man carrying a whip, with trousers tied just below the knees. This garment, however, had disappeared almost entirely by the turn of the century.

Fashionable material for female attire was lindsay, alpaca, flannel, cotton and print. Apart from the above mentioned everyday dress, some women also wore a plain skirt and bodice.

Edwin Grey in his "Cottage Life in a Hertfordshire Village", tells us that some of the very young girls had their Sunday dress made by a cottage dressmaker; other frocks would be "run up" at home, so that one can easily understand the answer of the little girl who, on being asked by her Sunday School teacher the question: "Who made your vile body?" replied, "Please, teacher, mother made the body but I made the skirt myself!"

Not many books were to be found in the village cottages. There might have been a few classics such as "Pilgrim's Progress", but one book was certain to be there, the Family Bible. Most of them were printed in large type, strongly bound in leather and the flyleaf would almost certainly contain a record of a family's history. Before the days of registering births and deaths, apart from Church registers,

▲
Schoolmistress Miss Randell in her 'Bath Chair'. She took over from the first schoolmistress, Miss Cundall. Note the Edwardian dress! JT

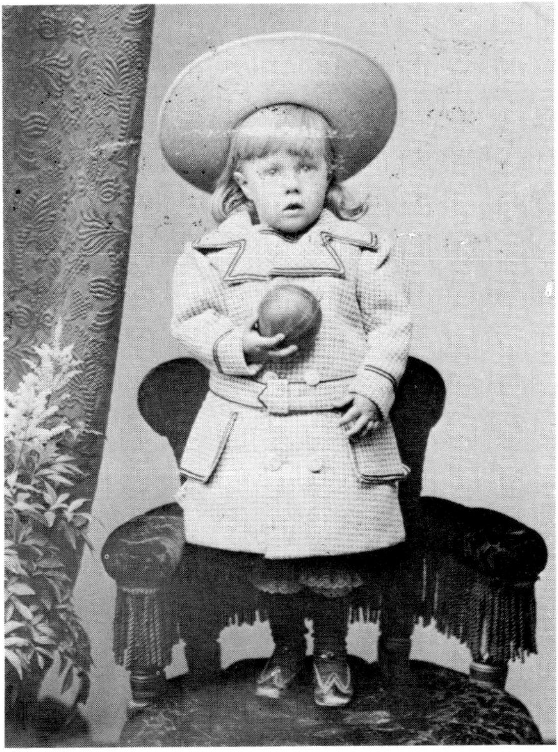

◀ *More female attire. Dressed up for a family portrait.*

◀ *Male attire from an earlier period, when, it has been suggested, the waistcoat was only taken off in bed! Such was its popularity.* JT

Female attire at the turn of the century. JT ▶

these entries were accepted as evidence if the need arose. Most Sunday evenings these Bibles would be fetched out and favourite stories read by a member of the family, and I have no doubt that in the period concerning us the bible stories were accepted implicitly. Edwin Grey tells us of an old lady who was asked if she really believed the story of Jonah and the whale. She replied that she did, and added that even if the Bible stated that Jonah had swallowed the whale, she would have believed that, too!

Village cottages, very attractive outside with their honeysuckle, jasmine, foxgloves and other traditional flowers, were usually sparsely furnished inside (though there were the exceptions, of course, with a few chairs, a stout table, and a mat in front of a range) this being the most important part of a room. Here the meals would be prepared using a large amount of wood to eke out the weekly hundredweight of coal, which cost a shilling.

If living rooms were sparsely furnished, the walls of the parlour certainly were not, often being adorned with a complete family history in pictures. And, of course, there was the piano around which the family would gather for an evening's entertainment.

Two old cottages. Changed now but still recognisable. The author's great-grandparents, Sam and Susan Bland, lived in the one on the left. Jack Farnham lives there now. BO

The cottages on the left stand in what were the grounds of a large house belonging to the Lilley Alchemist, the infamous Mr Johann Kellerman. BO

Frank Webb, the village shoe-mender, lived here with his mother and father. Typical village cottages. BO

An old cottage porch. Once a familiar sight in Lilley. JT

For economic reasons most families grew all their own vegetables and fruit. Both were of a first-rate quality, for our grandfathers really knew the value of manure, which they were able to obtain much more easily than we can today. The flower garden was often not much more than a strip at the side of the house, but what a profusion there would be: wallflowers and tulips, lavender and sweet william, pinks and perhaps an old-world rose, which could be either a moss rose, a monthly rose, a cabbage rose, a blood rose, or a big bush of the York and Lancaster rose, the blooms of which were mingled in a pied white and red.

Water was either drawn from a well, shared by a number of people or from a pump. For toilet purposes rainwater was drawn from a wooden butt outside the back door. After all, was it not good for the complexion?

In fine and warm weather most cottages could be seen with windows and doors wide open. After the morning housework, at such times, some women would sit outside the back door darning socks, making dresses or shirts and waistcoats for their often large families.

Unlike the false commercialism of today, Christmas at the time the new village church was being built was a simple, pleasurable festival. As far as I can ascertain, the "extras" at Christmas amounted to a joint of beef, often given by an employer to an employee, a plum pudding, a cake (not iced, but larger than normal) and perhaps apples saved from the garden trees. The children often received sweets for the festival. Not much by our standards, but their greater enjoyment lay, I think, around the family fireside, where children and grown-ups enjoyed good wholesome games, unlike many of us who sit and stare, glassy-eyed, at the "square box", winking and blinking at us like some garish monster, whose sole purpose is to lull us into a stupified state of inactivity.

The small cottages would be decorated with holly and evergreen, and perhaps there would be a small Christmas tree adorned with candles and other odds and ends obtained from the village shop for a halfpenny or a penny: a sheet of transfers with lions and tigers, a penny; a small packet of notepaper and envelopes, often pale blue or pale pink, decorated in a corner with a rose or a pansy, could be obtained for the same price; a small child's watch was another penny item. Then, of course, there were the sugar articles to be purchased for a very small amount, watches, lighthouses, churches, bells, houses and castles, trumpets, drums and fiddles, pink pigs and white mice and threepenny and fourpenny boxes of chocolates.

That delightful writer of country things, Alison Uttley, apart from mentioning the above articles for sale when she was a girl, gives some lovely little verses in her book, "Plowman's Clocks", which were often told around the fire at Christmas:

The mistletoe hung in the castle hall,
The holly branch shone on the old oak wall,
And the baron's retainers were blithe and gay
And keeping their Christmas holiday.
The baron beheld with a father's pride
His beautiful child, young Lovell's bride.

A Christmas Eve poem, which must be familiar to many elder folk, though I have never come across it myself, went:

'Twas the night before Christmas when all through
the house,
Not a creature was stirring, not even a mouse;
The stockings were hung by the chimney with care,
In hopes that Saint Nicholas soon would be there.

Alison Uttley continues:

> "The chapter on the Nativity was read to us, and we knelt down on the stone floor and said our Christmas Eve prayers. Then we went upstairs to the firelit bedrooms. The waifs were coming to sing carols in the yard. The angels were in the sky. The shepherds were in the hills. Christmas Day was very near ..."

All very lovely, but Alison Uttley was a farmer's daughter, and perhaps did not know the very real problem of feeding and clothing ten, eleven or even thirteen children; but, from every available source, it is also evident that despite their poverty people were happier; which seems to suggest that happiness depends more upon a state of mind, and body perhaps, than upon circumstances, possessions and events. On this assumption, the old ladies who lived in the village's almshouses were rich indeed!

The physique of the old craftsmen and their straw-plaiting wives — many, if not all, having now passed for the last time through the doors of the village church of St. Peter's — denoted the extreme hardships of their early lives. Men round-shouldered with spinal curvature due to hard work in early years before the bones were properly hardened; old men and women bent with rheumatism; angular development of limbs denoting under-nourishment; each were common and the accepted order of life.

To them we render our tribute of respect mingled with admiration; our thanks for a wonderful heritage that lies hidden in a small village threatened with losing its identity beneath the mayhem which is today's rat-race. Faithful to their simple order of life, they bravely won through in face of difficulties and hardship.

In comparative contrast between communal life then and now, there is perhaps no more outstanding feature of change than the degree to which the village of that day provided for its own requirements. Its tailors made the clothing, its bootmakers the shoes, boots and leggings, its wheelwrights the carts and wagons, the ploughmaker the wooden ploughs, its bakers the good wholesome bread, the blacksmith shoed the horses, the farm hands tilled the fields and the sawyer provided the planks and boards.

A place of much activity was the village sawyer's yard. Buying standing trees, he cut them down and stored them in the yard for twelve months. Then the sides of the logs were trimmed with an axe and afterwards rolled over the saw pit to be sawn by hand into boards or planks. These required some years of seasoning before they were considered fit for use.

Pit-sawing was very hard work, and no one that had ever undertaken it regretted for a moment its passing over to the machine, these at first being worked by steam. Such machines could be seen at Stopsley, where at least two village men, Arthur Tuttleby and Will Oliver, were employed.

Back at the hand sawyer's yard, piles of logs, rolled together, wait operations; a carpet of chips covers the ground and a fragrant smell of wood pervades all. A log is being prepared for sawing. George Barker, arms bared and shirt sleeves rolled over the elbows, wields a large bright axe, cleaving off huge chips and bark and leaving the grain of the wood showing bright and clean. A long string, soaked in black stain, is now strained from end to end of the log, and the lines of the boards and planks struck off. The log is then carefully rolled over the pit and wedged into position; after which sawing commences, two men wielding a huge long saw hour after hour, up and down, for several days.

Of the blacksmith we can read: "The labours of the Smith are highly to be prized, since every trade, more or less, is indebted to him." This is proved by some quotes from the accounts of Edward Cain, who had a little forge overlooking the village Green.

The account of D. Butterfield: "60 harrow tines laid, 7s 6d; 72 larg harrow tines, new laid, 12s; new bolt and nut altred to plow 2d; spindl kee, 2d; 1 larg link to middel chain, 3d; fork joind, mended 2 places, 6d; 1 link pin altred to cart, 3d; 1 new kee to card, 3d; rod joind, mended to plow, 5d; 6 new harrow tines, 4 new nuts, 3s; new irons to standard plow, 1s; new bit to kee, 4d; handl mended to drill, 6d; 2 bolts, joind to tap, 6d; plow winch joind, mended, 6d; plow picker joind, mended, new funnel put on, 9d."

J. Wilson: "4 new shoes to Gray nag, 2s 6d; new tine to fork, 5d; cuting knif ground, 3d; dung fork joind, mended, 5d; spout mended to drill, 4d; 4 shoes to the pony, 2s 2d; 9 pig rings, 6d; 2 links to chain, 2d; 1 stapl, 1d; turnup scip mended, 8d; new kee to copper doer put on, 8d; 2 handles put on a plow, 6d; new spring to rat trap, 5d; cog mended to drill, 6d; 2 hog rings, 2d; 2 tines mended, others altred put in horse drag, 1s 6d; new shank to stabl fork, 5d; 72 harrow tines, new laid 12s; new cupling and pin to harrow, 5d; 5 new rings, 2 bolts mended to harrow, pec (piece) of iron altred to Gat (gate) 3d; 2 new bolts and nuts to Boddey plait, 10d; 4 rings put on harnis, 8d."

Mrs. Russell, licensee of the Sowerby Arms: "Hiens (irons?) mended, 3d; charf knif ground, 3d; 1 link to coll rain (collar rein), 1d; 4 links to a chain and hook mended, 7d; new nut to plow harm, 5d; 4 shoes to the colt, 2s 8d." is followed by "8d for beer", which I can only interpret as meaning that Edward paid Mrs Russell for a fairish amount of good old English ale: "Youck mended, 4d" gives a picture of an attractive village maiden carrying a "yoke" of two buckets of milk, or am I letting my imagination run away with me? "New kee to box, 2d; new guggen (gudgeon) pin to wheelbarrow, 6d; new bolt and tap put on corn sifter, 2s; heg (hedge) chopper ground, 2d."

M. Snell, a builder, had "sixty revets for 9d; a new hook to pulleys for 5d, 2 new washers to hook, 2d, a chissel maid longr, 6d; 2 new irons to ladder, 1s; 18 nails maid longr, 1s 6d."

"New hook put on cart wheel" cost D. Davies 1s 6d; he paid 8d for a "new harf inch wassher"; 4d for "4 stapls to cart sharft" and 4d for "2 stapls altred sharft to cart".

Alfred Saunders, the village pig-sticker, paid 6d for having 12 long hooks made, and 3d for "loc altred to doer".

The licensee of the Red Lion, Arthur Toyer: "Stail put on 2 tind (two-tined) fork and revets, 5d; 4 pecs put on drill handl, 1s 6d; 6 pigs rung, 1s".

W. Ewer: "Four shoes to pone (pony), 2s; butt hoops mended, put on and spikes, 5d; nob to doer altred, 6d; handl joind to copper, 6d; milk pail mended, 3 places, 6d; a pair of heg clippers mended, new revet, 8d; new hook and ring to gait, 5d; hinge mended to greenhows, 4d".

Mr. Laird: "Two harrow biems (beams?) joind, mended, 10d." First mention of a water cart here: Two hoops were "put on warter cart hub" for a shilling.

It is very noticeable in these entries that if, for instance, a pail developed a hole or a water butt needed new hoops, they were not thrown out to litter the countryside, but taken for repair to the blackmsith and used again. Perhaps a blacksmith in every village now would help to solve our litter problem ... or have our personalities changed so much; are articles so easy to buy that we do not now value our possessions?

FARM WAGGON

CLAPPER USED FOR BIRD SCARING

PLOUGH

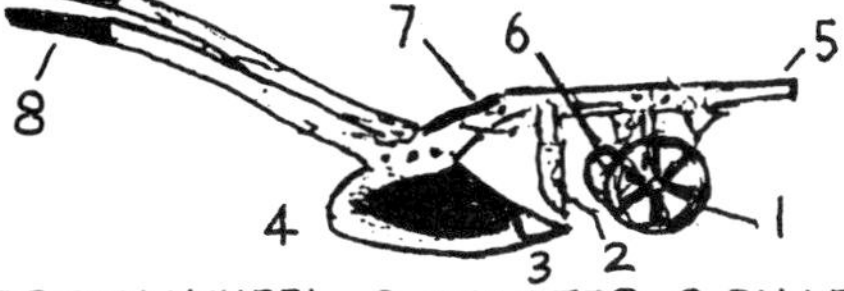

1 FURROW WHEEL 2 COULTER 3 SHARE 4 MOULD BOARD
5 HEAD 6 LAND WHEEL 7 BEAM 8 HANDLE

One cannot help a feeling of regret that the increasing use of machines is responsible for the disappearance of a good deal that was picturesque from the harvest field, and indeed from farm life generally.

The flail, which was used just within living memory, is now a museum piece. The skilful handling of the scythe as it passed with a swish through the ripened corn is rarely, if ever, seen; the enlivening sight of a team of horses drawing the reaping machine has disappeared, too. In fact, these fine and friendly animals are few and far between but are on the increase in places.

A TYPICAL VILLAGE WELL

SNUDGEL TO RETRIEVE BUCKET

YOKE AND WOODEN WELL BUCKET

The scythe gave place to the binder. Where once skilled man with a scythe would, under favourable conditions, mow about one acre per day, the tractor-drawn binder reaped and bound into sheaves fifteen or sixteen acres. The binder itself has now been outmoded by the combine harvester, which can deal with fifteen to twenty-five acres per day. What next I wonder?

Owing to the English climate it frequently happens that the grain is too moist for the miller when it leaves the combine. Means of drying must, therefore, be found, and this is provided on farms in the grain-drying plant.

The real old rustic — there are so few left now — the woodman, the blacksmith, the wheelwright, the gardener, to name but a few, had many words of his own; words that have almost disappeared from the countryside.

He had his "beaver" at mid-morning and in harvest time his "fourses" in the afternoon. For his mid-day meal of bread and meat, often salt pork, the meat was placed on about half a loaf of bread and a small piece of bread known as a "thumb piece" was used to hold the meat while it was cut with a horn-handled pocket knife.

If he had a penny in the evening, this was a "latch-lifter", that is, sufficient money for half a pint, which would pay his way into the inn, after which he could hope for someone else to pay for another drink. He smoked thick twist in a "nose-warmer", a clay pipe, sold for a farthing, broken off about two inches from the bowl. The way home was by the "twitchell", a narrow path, and if he thought of ghosts he might be "near frit to death". During the day he would "lim into it" (work hard) and "do his whack" (do his share of the work). Anyone hurrying would be described as "clarrin' about", though he might not get much "forrader" by his effort.

Allotments were known as "garden fields" and a good summer rain after a dry spell was a "good tater rain", one that soaked down to the potatoes. Mangles were known as "wozzles" and hay was carted in a "tumble cart with copses on", the copse being the rack put on the back and front of the cart to increase the loading space. Beating the walnut tree to bring down the nuts was known as "splashing walnuts".

In the building trade, a carpenter would say, after fixing a piece of wood: "That's as firm as a church tied to a hedge". Another, describing a hard piece of timber, would say: "It's as hard as a brazeel" (this may have meant a brazil nut). A soft piece would be: "As soft as a carrot". The same man, training an apprentice, would tell him: "the old-fashioned way's the best, hit 'em on the head", when driving in nails; or "Don't sow 'em, they won't grow", when the lad dropped a few; or "Fetch yer mother" if he was stuck over some little job.

A joiner's router was known as an "old woman's tooth" or a "granny's tooth", and was generally a home-made one. A whipple-tree was the term for a yoke on a two-horse cart, but the same term was used when making window frames. A bricklayer, constructing a flat brick arch, would always count the bricks to determine whether it was a "he" or a "she". An odd number of bricks with a central key brick, made a "he".

A hundred-odd years ago, the ordinary farm worker earned only a few shillings a week, and the majority of boys went to village farms as "backhouse boys" and earned perhaps two shillings a week. These boys sometimes slept at the farms, but had to find the greater part of their own food which, although coming to them from home when possible, meant they very often knew what it was to go hungry. Some of the lads would go to the Michaelmas hiring fair at Luton, where they could be taken on for a year by neighbouring farmers at low weekly wages with a lump sum payment at the end of their year's contract. It is easy to see that although they were employed they were not necessarily helping to support their families, indeed they must at times have been a burden. Girls, too, often left home to work as maids. To go into "service" was considered the "thing" for most village girls.

It is not surprising, therefore, that a vast number of households had a job to make ends meet. Fortunately, there was another industry available which enabled wives and even some of the men to supplement the family income. In those days, many straw hats were fashioned from hand-made English plait, and it was a common sight in the village to see little clusters of neighbours having a gossip while their nimble fingers plaited the straw into various designs.

In summer, women and girls, such as Rose Roffe, Etty Payne, Liz Allen and Betsy Watson, walked around the village or sat on stiles and gates or on the grass plaiting; links of plait over their left arms, a dampened bunch of straws with a brown paper damp-proof cover under the same arm. In winter, they sat round the fire in their cottage homes, plaiting and reading or plaiting and singing; often during the winter evenings men plaited as well. This was the age, too — before the Compulsory Education Act of 1870 — of the plait school, where for perhaps a penny a week children were supposed to be taught to read and write and to plait, though one suspects it was the latter subject that was considered the most important one. In the village, Church Cottage was once a such a school. There may have been others as well.

The process of straw plait making began when the straw dealers purchased the unthreshed wheat stacks from the farmers, at a cost varying from £5 to £10 a ton. When the straw had been put into the barn the dealer or his men selected the best and longest stems, cut off the ears and tied the straws up into half-cut or one-cut bundles for sale; or they might be "stripped", that is, cut to remove the knots and leaf, leaving the straws nine to ten inches long. This was often done by piecework, quantity being determined by filling a pottle measure.

The straws were then bleached in a closed box into which molten sulphur had been introduced, and sometimes dyed, although in the early days the range of colours was very limited. Grading into the various thicknesses was done with the aid of a straw sorter, a wooden frame into the top of which was fitted a series of wire sieves of various meshes. A handful of straws was jolted loosely over each mesh in turn, working from the finest to the coarsest, the appropriate straws falling through into boxes below. They were then tied into bundles five or six inches in diameter and sold to the plaiters by the straw dealers, either in the markets or from door to door.

Plaiting: The plaiter worked with a bundle of straws or "splints" under her left arm, drawing out new straws as needed, and passing them between her lips to moisten them before using. Plaits were made with varying numbers of "ends" (straws in use simultaneously), usually ranging from three to seven, and as their length was only nine to ten inchess long new ones had to be introduced at regular intervals, leaving small portions of the heads and tails of the straws projecting from the plait — the "set-ins" and the "speel" — to be clipped off afterwards. The basic plaiting operation needs little description; it consisted of a regular over-and-underlocking of the straws, which in the simplest patterns were folded back flatly when the edge of the plait was reached; but there were many variations to produce other patterns of plait.

Plait was measured up into "tens" (half-score) or "scores" of yards, usually by the simple method of winding it between finger and thumb and under the elbow; then tied up into bundles of 40 or 50 scores.

The Straw-Splitter: When efforts were made to produce plait fine enough to compete with the Italian product by using split straws, it is probable that at first the splitting was done with a knife. Later, a special tool, the straw splitter, was used. Some had individual handles and some were inserted in sets into small wooden frames, but the cutting principle was the same for all: a point of metal or bone with blades varying from three to twelve or thirteen, arranged radially around the neck. The straw was placed over the point and pressed forward until it engaged the blades, which cut it into a number of even-sized "splints".

The Plait: Plaits made with whole straws were known as "Wholestraw Plaits", the simplest types being made by the basic method mentioned and called 3-ends Plain, 5-ends Plain, 7-ends Plain, Twist Wholestraw, etc., and some remarkable fine whole-straw plaits were produced by using bents, i.e. the stems of grasses. Plaits made with splints, or split straws were known as "Split Plait".

They were of five, seven, eleven or thirteen ends, and finer and lighter than wholestraw plaits, but had the disadvantage of showing the outside, or "shiny" and the inside or "nice" alternatively as the straws were turned over in plaiting.

Certain districts specialised in a particular type of plait. According to Austin, the Luton historian, Hitchin and Biggleswade produced broad and medium twists, Shefford narrow twist, Ampthill narrow improved, Houghton Regis Devon and fine split, Eaton Bray twist and coloured plait, Ivinghoe rustic and narrow twist, Chesham Devon and fine split, moss edge and Vienna, Berkhamsted China purl, rock and Coburg, St. Albans twists, Devons and improved, Breachwood Green, Offley and Lilley plain and twist wholestraw.

Milling: Before they were plaited the straws or splints were flattened by being passed through a "splint-mill", a small mangling device, generally of beechwood or boxwood rollers. They were usually screwed to the cottage doors, the operation often being the job of children. A "plait mill" of similar construction was used for flattening and making more pliable the finished plait. The rollers were, however, grooved into "trolls" to take various widths of plait, with a smaller and deeper groove on one side of each troll to take the fancy heads of the plait and allow them to escape the pressure exerted on the remainder.

The complete plait was sold either to travelling agents; at Luton Plait Market, or at —

Hitchin Plait Market. Imagine a November morning in 1897. The church tower of St. Mary's stands gaunt and sturdy against the grey sky. The air is damp cold, but the citizens of the old market town are already bustling about in anticipation of a good day's trade. Cattle, being driven in from surrounding villages, blunder, a little frightened perhaps, on to the pavements to avoid the countless carts piled high with bags of plait straw, or of produce from neighbouring smallholdings. Among the cattle struggle men and women, carrying completed plait for sale in the market.

The clock of the ancient parish church strikes a quarter to nine. Already the stalls are loaded with bags into which are packed bunches of straws cut into nine-inch lengths of varying sizes. The pavement round the four sides of Market Square is fringed with women and a few men, hands clasped, their arms festooned with links of plait, each link a yard in length and tied with string in ten-yard lengths.

Buying and selling is illegal until nine o'clock, but a few men can be seen sauntering round the square, as if inspecting the plait, but signalling with their fingers. Eight fingers and a thumb signifying ninepence for a score yards of plait. For one old lady this is not enough, she turns her head towards the church — the signal of refusal. Another dealer indicates "eleven", the old woman nods agreement. Suddenly, the figures, straw and all, come to life. The uniformed bellman has clanged his bell; the church clock echoes the last stroke of nine; all is clatter, laughter, argument and shouting. Another market is open.

The womenfolk are well wrapped against the cold, most in coats of a dark material, some in brighter checks. Nearly all wear hats: big hats, small hats, smart hats and plain hats. A few shawls can be seen amongst the milling crowd, and with neck-scarves make a bright splash on this drab morning. The shops around the square are dwarfed, perhaps insignificant, on this market day; straw plait and garden produce are the things that matter now. The day wears on. A watery sun throws a few futile beams of light across the canvas stall-tops, then slips, like a sinking ship in a black sea, behind the horizon. The crowds drift away. The stalls are taken down. All is quiet. Rose Roffe, Etty Payne and Betsy Watson wend their way, a little weary now, down Sun Street, up Tilehouse Street, along Offley Road, and then home.

Old local newspapers are invaluable if a person is seeking to trace the history and life of a town. Likewise, old parish magazines help us to trace the past life, the hopes and fears, of a parish; in this case, a village. Looking through one such publication for 1891, I came across an item from which one gathers it was a general custom for a parson to "shepherd" his flock through the medium of his magazine; to "suggest" which direction they should take in such a way that the reader was left in little doubt as to whom the message was directed.

A little word in kindness spoken,
  A motion or a tear,
Has often healed the heart that's broken,
  And made a friend sincere.
A word — a look — has crushed to earth
  Full many a budding flower,
Which, had a smile but owned its birth,
  Would bless life's darkest hour.
Then deem it not an idle thing
  A pleasant word to speak;
The face you wear, the thought you bring,
  A heart may heal or break.

"All is not attractive that is good. Iron does not sparkle like a diamond, yet it is useful. Gold has not the fragrance of a flower, yet it is valuable. So different persons have different graces of excellence.

"He who never changed any of his opinions never corrected any of his mistakes; and he who was never wise enough to find out any mistakes in himself will not be charitable enough to excuse what he reckons mistakes in others."

The winter of 1892 saw an outbreak of 'flu, which caused the death of the young Duke of Clarence, the elder son of the Prince and Princess of Wales, and proved to be something of a scourge locally. A parish magazine for that year reported:

"When one feels a quick pulse, burning hands and head, a splitting headache, a continued shivering, aching joints, a feeling of giddiness with a hard, dry cough, then it is about time to go to bed and send for a doctor."

"What the complaint is and where it comes from, no one can tell. It is in many respects like the old-fashioned 'Shaky Ague', which has disappeared with the better drainage of modern times, but that did not affect the lungs as this does, and it is just because its effects on the lungs are so serious that it is necessary to take the very greatest care, both at the commencement and during the continuance of the illness. Keep as much as possible in one temperature: don't attempt to go to work too soon, and above all things, avoid stimulants, and drink as much milk and beef-tea as you can get."

On the subject of cleanliness, a writer in a magazine for 1895 gave some advice on spring cleaning and personal hygiene:

"That dirt encourages vermin, both in houses and on the person, is certain. Keep the house clean, and if possible, whitewash it every year. You will then be but little troubled with those pests which destroy rest and irritate the skin and the temper at the same time. Whitewashing, or rather lime-washing, is an easy process and nothing has so good an effect in destroying the germs of insect life and of disease.

"Try, then, when the spring cleaning comes round, when 'that nasty sun which shows up all the cobwebs' begins to shine strongly, to give walls and ceilings a wholesome dose of limewash; even the floors will be all the better and sweeter if cleaned with some of the clear water which stands at the top after the lime has settled. If you have a garden, turn out all your beds and mattresses, beat and brush them well, and then let them lie in the sun and fresh air, getting soaked with purity; in fact, till the room is dry and fit to receive them again. You will have all the sweeter sleep because the beds have had their sunbath."

On the question of personal hygiene, the writer makes the point that the dwellings of the poor had neither bathrooms or the convenience of a big washtub, which could be found in the homes of the wealthy, but they could still be clean. He advocated a washing-pan, a piece of stout flannel, in preference to a sponge, and a piece of soap. "A very small outlay will give us these", he said, "and how much comfort and pleasure do we derive from them! ... and even if shut off from the big tub and the large quantity of water, we may all daily indulge in a wash from head to foot."

Seventy-five years ago The Church Monthly printed an article about courtship and marriage. It contained the story of an old rustic who said to a friend: "If everyone had been of my mind, everyone would have wanted to marry my old woman." His friend replied: "If everyone had been of my mind no one would have wanted to marry her."

The article goes on to relate a few hints when considering marriage: "First of all, it is unwise to choose a life partner for beauty alone. After the first year married people rarely think of each other's features: and whether they are classically beautiful or otherwise becomes a matter of small moment. But they never fail to be cognisant of each other's character, and especially of temper. Domestic habits, too, belong to the class of essentials. You do not want a partner who may be found anywhere except at home, or one who, when at home, can and will do nothing to make it comfortable."

"How to be happy though married" took a humorous if somewhat sarcastic look at the problems of married and family life. About bringing up children, the author had this to say: 1. Begin young by giving him whatever he cries for. 2. Tell him he is too much for you — that you can do nothing with him. 3. Have divided counsels as between father and mother. 4. Let him learn (from his father's example) to despise his mother. 5. Do not know or care who his companions may be. 6. Let him read whatever he likes. 7. Let the child, whether boy or girl, roam the streets in the evenings — a good school for both sexes. 8. Strain at a gnat and swallow a camel: Chastise severely for an accident, and laugh at a fault. These rules are not untried. Many parents have proved them, with substantial uniformity of results. If a faithful observance of them does not spoil your child, you will have had at least the comfortable reflection that you have done what you could!"

Poultry-keeping as a profitable hobby was the subject of a small article by a Vicar. He extolled the virtues of keeping chickens, making the whole thing sound as easy as ABC. One had only to pick up a book, build a run in the garden, buy some birds, and hey-presto it was done!

"There never was a time when such facilities were offered for acquiring knowledge as the present. If knowledge is power, then that power is offered even to the humblest and weakest ... books were never less costly, newspapers never cheaper, nor more abundant. There is scarcely a technical subject on which information is desired, but a home instructor can be supplied at the small cost of one penny weekly.

"But surely with all these aids at our command there ought to be in process of formation such a race of amateur carpenters, woodcarvers, gardeners, poultry-keepers, bee-keepers, etc., as England has never seen the like of before. Means are now at our disposal whereby urban and rural dweller alike can turn the hours of leisure to a practical and profitable use. This is a great stride over the supposed attractions of the public house, the penny sing-song, and the weak and washy penny readings.

"It would be hard indeed to find any better means of teaching people how to help themselves than by poultry-keeping. The facilities are usually at command, the outlay is small, the return comes quickly, the occupation is healthy; buyers are not difficult to find, and with care and attention a balance can easily be shown on the right side. The waste food of the home will go a long way towards feeding a few fowls. Corn, which must be bought, was never cheaper than today, whilst on the other hand the prices realised for eggs and poultry were never higher. Surely a favourable moment this for embarking in a fascinating occupation.

In 1885, many branches of a society called The Primrose League were formed. It originated "to keep alive in the hearts of Englishmen the memory and principles of the great Conservative leader, Lord Beaconsfield, whose favourite flower was the primrose".

All members of the League were "required to promise that they will maintain the constitution of England, as it stands at present, viz: the Queen, the House of Lords, and the House of Commons. That they will support national morality by the maintenance of religion, and that they will, wherever necessity arises, defend the honour and integrity of the British Empire".

In April, 1886, a local speaker had something to say about women and politics. He found it rather puzzling, he said, to address a meeting composed of women as well as men; though it was well the women should take an interest in politics, he did not think it would be desirable they should have votes, they might be led to neglect home duties!" What would he say today, I wonder?

He continued: "Married women should try to make their husbands' homes comfortable, and those who have no husband as yet should try to save their money, and not spend it on fine bonnets, so that when they do marry they will have something to begin upon."

The Quiver magazine for 1881 ran a serial called "In Vanity and Vexation", with a heroine named Kythe Anstey. Looking through these stories gives a very good idea of the attitude to life of those times.

The story starts with a description of a farmhouse kitchen in which Kythe had just arrived: The broad cavernous fireplace would be what is now the fashionable inglenook; the dresser (of the Welsh variety, no doubt) rich in old china and brilliant with polished tins and coppers; in the centre of the room a long table, and seated there, at the further end, a little removed from the rough labourers, with the clay of the fields on their garments, and the ruddy bare-armed women servants, two persons whose dress and demeanour distinguished them from the rest.

At the rear end of the table stood a typical housekeeper of the period: Tall, stout, forbidding, in coarse bibbed apron and holland sleeves, hewing off huge slices of salt pork with a careful but generous hand, taking good care that an equal share of pudding was given to each diner, but administering at the same time sundry lectures on the sinfulness of waste and gluttony. This good person very soon took a dislike to Kythe for her attire: The beaded trimmings on her hat, the spotted veil, a feather curling over the brim, a fringe of wavy hair across the forehead — a fashion so detestable to the housekeeper that she had summarily dismissed a dairymaid for adopting it — kid gloves; expensive articles of attire that ought not to be donned except on fine Sundays and high-day visits to the market. I guess she might have forty-thousand fits today!

In 1822, Sir Robert Peel became Home Secretary. he proved to be an enlightened and liberal administrator. At that time the criminal law was in need of reform. The penalty of death was inflicted for hundreds of offences which were called "felonies". This excessive severity — which Dickens illustrates so well and under which many were hanged for thefts prompted, not by a criminal intent, but by a social evil that allowed three-quarters of the population to exist at barely starvation level, while the remainder lived in comparative luxury — sometimes defeated its own object, for some felonies were of so trivial a character that juries were reluctant to convict persons charged with minor crimes for which the punishment was so terrible.

Peel removed more than a hundred offences from the list of capital crimes, and thus began a reform which in a few years left the death penalty applicable to only four crimes — murder, treason, piracy and setting fire to a royal dockyard. In 1829 he established the Metropolitan Police, a well-trained and highly efficient force which was in course of time imitated in all parts of the country. In 1840, Hertfordshire adopted the County Police Act, but even then village constables were appointed on a temporary basis by the annual Vestry meeting. In addition, of course, there were the Bow Street Runners, who, in 1811 were concerned in a local happening involving a band of poachers calling themselves the Hexton Archers.

Local landowners, it appears, headed by Sir Francis de Latour, being the chief victims of nightly forays, arrayed their gamekeepers in opposition. But the poachers, desperate no doubt to maintain their supply of food and well disciplined to the point of military precision in their use of bows and arrows, caused such casualties among them as to deter even the most foolhardy of gamekeepers. In sheer desperation and anguish, Sir Francis at last appealed to the Bow Street Runners for help. Early in December that year Terence Brady, a man as equally well-disciplined and determined as the poachers, arrived on the scene.

The weeks that followed saw this Chiltern valley turned into a battlefield, with Brady pitting his skill against a leader of exceptional brilliance and cunning. Fires were lit, hayricks, barns and even isolated cottages were fired in attempts to draw Brady's attention while raids took place elsewhere. When this plan failed small groups of poachers sought out his force and engaged them in fierce running fights.

After almost a month Brady had achieved very little so decided to operate alone. Despite the entreaties of the landowners, he set up a lonely vigil in a tree overlooking the village and on the second night his patience was rewarded. Noting a man cautiously leave his house under the cover of darkness, Brady decided to follow him.

Unwittingly, his quarry led him to the gang's meeting place.

Along the road towards Hitchin stands the Live and Let Live, a small inn reputedly deriving its name from the incident which found some fifty men besieged within while sharing out the spoils of their escapades. Brady took them unawares. With twenty armed and determined men surrounding the place, he called upon the inmates to surrender. They refused.

Brady then played a cunning, but nevertheless brilliant trick on the poachers. He ordered his men to dismantle a nearby hayrick, piling the bundles about the walls of the inn; then in full view of the beleaguered inmates he set fire to it. The ruse worked. Believing the officer intended to burn them alive, the poachers quickly threw down their arms and ran through the billowing black smoke in surrender.

First mention of a constable here can be found in records for 1835, when at a Vestry meeting on April 29, Edward Gray was granted a new pair of handcuffs. The following year, on March 25, it became necessary to appoint two constables — Jas. Attwood and William Robinson. A new pair of handcuffs and two constables suggests, perhaps, that crime was rife in the village a hundred and fifty years ago. We do know that at this time there was a stock-house outside the church gates, and the Rector was a JP, so it is easy to imagine that swift justice was the rule here, with constant occupants of the stocks.

Constables normally served for twelve months, sometimes only for six, and it appears to have been a duty that was generally shirked by those public-minded gentlemen who made up the village Vestry. What qualifications were needed is not stated, but I imagine one would need to be of a tough disposition!

On December 10, 1839, the Vestry resolved "it is not expedient to establish a Rural Police in this Parish according to the Act". Which is surprising, when one considers that being a constable appeared to be such an irksome task, but no doubt their sense of duty to the village's ratepayers was stronger than their own personal feelings, so the proposal received no support here. However, the matter was taken out of their hands in 1840 when a county and rural force was organised.

April, 1841, saw Captain Archibald Robertson, from Scotland, appointed Hertfordshire's first Chief Constable. When he took charge of the county force he had under him four superintendents, six inspectors and sixty constables, and the annual estimated cost was £5,200.

Not everyone could qualify for membership of the county police in those days any more than they can now, but it was not a force noted for its strong physique, for the average height was five feet seven and three-quarter inches. Some were as small as five feet six inches and very few were over six feet tall. But they had to be men of intelligence and strength of character. Discipline, which today would be tiresome, was cheerfully accepted.

No member of the force could keep a dog, pig or fowl or any description of livestock. Constables were not allowed to leave home without permission in between periods of duty.

Married officers were given a concession. They could accompany their wives and families to Divine Service in plain clothes, but if going alone they had to wear uniform. During off-duty hours on Sunday, constables could accompany their wives and families for a walk in plain clothes, providing the walk did not last more than two hours and that there was a person who could receive messages during the constable's absence.

Four part-time constables were elected in the village in 1869: William Cain, Alfred Saunders, William Ewer and Roger Irons; four more in 1870, 1871; and in 1872 it was recorded: "In public vestry assembled this day pursuant to legal notice thereof for the purpose of nominating Constables of this Parish for the ensuing year: Alfred Saunders, Francis Allingham, William Ewer and Shadrick Atkins were nominated to serve the office for the year ensuing."

In 1890, it was decreed that no full-time constable should be allowed to marry unless he possessed furniture to the value of £20 or that sum in cash. Receipts, bank books and other documents had to be produced. The first uniform was top hat and tailed coat, but in 1891 this was changed to helmet and tunic.

Police pay in 1880 was: Superintendents £115 per year, sergeants 27s per week, constables 21s per week; and when 12 constables went off to fight in the Boer War their wives received 10s a week with 1s 6d. for each child under 15. In 1881, it was ordered that every sergeant and constable should attend church once every Sunday wearing uniform. One week's annual leave with pay and a day off per month instead of one day every three months was granted in 1897.

Each customer of the village's three inns had his own favourite spot in the taproom, near the bar, or near the fire, on bench or chair. Here he would have his half-pint for a penny and his pipeful of shag tobacco. Usual topics of conversation would be local happenings: cricket, parish council affairs, the squire, or perhaps religion — and, of course, the weather!

Imagine yourself in the Lilley Arms one night. The evening was hot and sultry. The door to the taproom opens and in walks a real old rustic wearing the largest and heaviest pair of hop-nailed boots you ever saw. His chief topic of conversation was the state of the weather, with rain as its sole theme. He greeted Jack Stormer, the landlord, something like this: "We doan't git that there rain, Jack. Everythink'll be droid up, mark moi words! Thar'll be no wozzles or nothink else. Whoi, moi marrer bed's as droi as bloody charf, so it is." Another local worthy, sitting in the corner, might say: "Silly ol' bugger! 'E'll die o' warter on the brain, oi rackon."

When the rain did come it came well and truly. Day after day it poured and poured. Our friend with water on the brain clumped into the bar one evening: "We're a'gittin' too much rain now, Jack. Everythink'll be bloody soaked an' rotten. Them thar wozzles up at Sowerbys wun't be no good at arl; an' arl the ground's loike a sodding river, so it is!" The other worthy who had previously prophesied that our hero would die of water on the brain was not present, but another local, sitting nearby, obviously having similar opinions, muttered: "Barmy ol' bugger! Rain'll be the death o' 'im!"

An old cottage in Lilley being re-thatched. It was here that Bob Earl lived. He was reputed to be able to charm away warts.

An old gentleman, sipping from a tankard, told of a certain cure for warts: "If yew're plagued w' warts", he said, "yew git 'old o' a bit o' steak or cat's meat, lay it on the warts fer 'bout foive minutes, then take an' bury it 'gin the foot o' a blackthorn bush. They ol' warts'll be gorn afore the week's out, yew see if they doan't."

His companion maintained that to walk beneath a reared ladder without crossing the first and second fingers of each hand is courting trouble. "Whoi", he remarked, "oi once walked under a ladder, an' the very next day lorst a good litter o' pigs, an' arl because oi fergot to crorse me fingers! Yew take moi tip, marster, an' alwis crorse yer fingers under a ladder!"

Parish councils have a reputation for lengthy sittings at some of their meetings, and one village known to us all is no exception. A local character, propping up the bar, expressed this opinion of the parish council in no uncertain manner: "There they sat in that there Reading Room chapsing 'alf the noight, an' when they've finished 'arping they ai'nt said nothing! Look at that there footpath as they keep on 'bout ... meetin' arter meeting' they've 'ad an' got nowhere. Chaps, chaps, chaps, that's all they can do!" (The expressions "chaps" and "harp" mean unnecessary talking — Author.)

Old village folk always display a marvellous knowledge of weather conditions and changes. A remark to a local that it was a beautiful evening could bring a reply something like this: "Arr, thar'll be rain afore midnight, yew see if thar ain't!" And if one dares to say: "Why? There's not a cloud in the sky", he would regard you with contempt; his blue eyes would take on the faraway expression that one often sees in a person who for years has scanned the horizon; then the clay pipe is slowly taken from his mouth, to be clutched in a bony hand, beaten into tough leather by the elements, that points way down the Green Lane. "Wot 'bout they ol' 'erring-bones over yonder? An' see how they ol' starlins keeps a-swoopin' down. Thar'll be rain afore long, yew mark moi words!"

A certain old gentleman who once lived in our village but who, for obvious reasons, must remain anonymous, once had this to say about superstition: "Superstition? Doan't yew talk t' me 'bout superstition. If yew warn't t' know anythink 'bout superstition. If yew warn't t' know anythink 'bout that yew warn't t' 'ear 'bout ol' Tat. Whoi, a more superstitious man oi've never come acrorst. If ever 'e see ol' Mother Bland a'sitting at 'er front door with 'er black cat in 'er lap 'e'd run a moile the other way: moind yew, she did look a bit loike a witch, oi must say. If 'e saw a wall-eyed man (a disease of the eye in which the iris is of a very light grey or whitish colour — Author) 'e'd git the jim-jams an' neck a couple o' points in as many minutes. But what 'e wus more superstitious 'bout was the toime, 'E'd got a 'orrer o' arr-past eight, an' arl a'corse 'is farther doid at arr-past eight, an' so did 'is mother. 'E wus caught a'layin' rabbit snares at arr-past eight one noight ... 'ad up for it an' arl 'ewus. Next thing, 'is ol' grandfather clock stopped at arr-past eight, an' wou'nt gew agin f' arl the windin'. Then, t' crown it arl, 'e wus a'thatchin' a rick one day when oi'm blest if 'e dint fall orf an' break 'is leg; an' believe me or not, the toime wus arr-past eight! An' when ol' Happy arsked 'im if it wus in the bloody marnin' or at bloody noight, dang me if 'e dint call 'im arl the names under the sun as 'e could lay 'is tongue to!"

Old superstitions, in fact, were rife among village folk of a century ago, and even today some people still think it bad luck to put shoes on a table, or to drive a nail in wood on Good Friday, to name but two.

It was thought to be very bad luck to meet a piebald pony or horse. If one did meet such an animal, then the remedy was to cross one's feet and this would ward off the ill-luck; it was considered wicked to point at the moon, which heavenly planet was always referred to in a subdued voice. Why, is not quite clear.

Bees were considered to have some sort of magical power, and were kept informed of day to day events, preferably at evening time when they were all at home. If a person died the bees were informed of this, too, lest they all died as well. A small piece of crepe was fixed to the hive as a sign of mourning.

It was thought that if a bride stepped from the church porch with the left foot first she would always be under the thumb of her husband. Many brides, if this were true, must have put left foot first up to a decade or two ago, for undoubtedly at the turn of the century the man was "master".

Pebbles known as "God stones" carried in a pocket were supposed to bring good luck, and a potato carried likewise would ward off rheumatism.

The weather has always been a favourite subject with English people, so it is understandable that it should be associated by the townsman with superstition. I would prefer the word "lore" to "superstition", which means a misplaced belief. The old country beliefs about the weather have proved time and again not to be misplaced.

Perhaps this is because so many country people depended on the weather for their livelihood. They studied its moods and vagaries, its association with birds, the movement of cloud and direction of wind, and could, and some can still, give a more accurate forecast than the "Met" with verses thus:

When the wheel is far the storm is n'ar.
When the wheel is n'ar the storm is far.

Another:

> Mackerel sky and mare's tails,
> Make tall ships carry low sails.

And:

> Rain before seven, fine before eleven

is a saying still in vogue today, and is explained by low pressure troughs which take roughly four hours to pass. Fine weather follows when the barometer rises, which takes place when the low trough has passed. Logical, isn't it?

> A red sky at night is the shepherd's delight,
> A red sky in the morning is the shepherd's warning.

> Where the wind is on Candlemas Day,
> There it will stick till the Second of May.

> A wet March makes a sad harvest.

> A peck of March dust is worth a king's ransom.

> As many mists in March, so many frosts in May.

> There are many more, enough probably to fill a book.

Chapter 5

Mainly Topographical

The name Lilley is probably derived from the old English Lin-leah — a clearing where flax was grown. In the Domesday Survey it is spelt Linleia, where it is stated "There are 19 villeins and a priest". In 1204 the spelling was Lin-lege, and in 1212 Lin-lee.

In 1302 comes the name William de Ward, still echoed today in Wards Farm, Wards Wood Lane and most likely Warden Hills and Wards Spring. It seems obvious that Wards Wood Lane once joined the Icknield Way to enable drovers to drive their livestock to the Fountain public house with its large meadow land and sleeping accommodation.

There is a section of Wards Wood Lane or Green Lane that is much more narrow than the rest. This begins at a point where a cart track descends from Wards Farm to the lane. This narrow section is remembered as a rutted high banked piece of track where livestock could not stray and was known as Lumber Lane, but it seems most likely this began as Number Lane, a place where the livestock could be driven through a few at a time and counted.

The almshouses were a row of small cottages next to the Silver Lion beside what is now the A505, and administered, it seems, by the squire. The occupants were charged one shilling a week for the privilege of living in the cottages, and lest anyone should forget they were in receipt of charity the old ladies always wore red shawls when venturing out. Three of the occupants still remembered today were Eliza Webb, Edie Coles and Betsy Watson.

Whilst in this vicinity, a happening every week that could, and probably did, have interesting consequences, took place on Mondays and latterly Tuesdays for years and years on the road from Hitchin to Luton, namely the cattle that were driven from Hitchin Market to Luton for slaughtering. With a man at the back and perhaps another at the front, it must have been quite a headache preventing the cattle straying into gardens, backyards and up alleyways. On one occasion a beast decided to lie down right in the middle of the former Beech Hill ... it took nearly a whole day to move it!

At the turn of the century, when the village was practically a self-contained unit; when people were born, worked, married and died within its bounds, there were seven shops: At the top of the village was Lawrence's general shop; "Lennie", as he was affectionately known, son of the original owner, was quite famous in the area for his straw beehives, and although over 80 and stone-deaf, at the time of writing still walked the five miles to Hitchin Market; next came a butcher's shop kept by Charles Young, father of Arthur Young, well-known village character for many years. Charles was quite handy on the big bass drum, and once a year headed a hired band through the village to attend the Foresters' Club Feast, which was held in a barn at Pond Farm.

The local pig-killer was "Shaddy" Saunders, who lived in a yard bearing his name; killed his own pigs, as well as other people's, and also sold brawn and lard. Next to "Shaddy" was Lizzie Cain's general shop. Wife of the celebrated Jabez, who owned the "Lilley Bus", she also sold pork pies. Then came Keeling's general store and Trussell's bakery. In 1900 Harry Trussell was the baker. His business was on one side of the village street and his home on the other, in

A background of elm trees, all now lost through Dutch Elm Disease. The old village butchers' shop can just be seen in the building on the right. BO

Part of the village green. The building on the left shows where the old Reading Room adjoined it. This is also where John 'Snob' Sansom was a cobbler.

A quiet summer scene in the middle of Lilley in the 1950s. Webb's General Store can be seen to the left. At one time this was the village post office. This was also the site of the former Red Lion public house; Keeling's general store and Trussell's bakery. BO

the meadow opposite the old school, where he lived with his mother. Harry had five brothers and three sisters: Ernie, Frank, Arthur, Walter (a tailor at Stevenage) and the Rev. David Trussell (the village school's most famous pupil), Annie, Bessie and Maggie (a teacher at Lilley school), described by the late Will Oliver as a lovely girl with the most beautiful complexion. Said Will: "We boys used to look forward to a clout from her!" Next to Trussell's was the post office, kept by Fred Godfrey, a staunch Methodist and a school governor.

As well as the seven shops there used to be Albert Toyer, the Blacksmith; Jesse Webb, a part-time Cobbler; John "Snob" Sansom, a full-time Cobbler; two lady Dressmakers, the Misses Thompson; and a Laundry kept by Miss Taylor.

Away over to the east, behind Church Farm, lies a large pit locally known as "The Lime Kiln". In the eighteenth century, large quantities of lime were spread on the fields and even larger quantities were used for mortar. Our church records show that in Lilley several bushels of lime were purchased two or three times a year, and "The Lime Kiln" is obviously the spot where this lime was burnt.

A man called Kalm, friend of William Ellis, a Hertfordshire farmer and prolific writer of the eighteenth century, while staying at Little Gaddesden with Ellis, described the process of how lime was burned from chalk:

"Here was an ordinary walled kiln in which bricks are burned. In it bricks and lime are burned together and at the same time. The chalk is first dug up in large or smaller pieces out of the chalk hills and is carried to the brick-kiln. Then, when one wishes to burn bricks, the kilns are walled over nearest to the fire with bare chalk, and in that quantity which one wishes to have of lime or of chalk, but not more than that the bricks also may be burned through.

"The largest pieces of chalk are laid nearest the fire and the smaller ones on top. Above the chalk are laid the bricks, which are burned in the usual way. After that a fire is made in the kiln pipes, in which there were two. First of all, large wood is laid in, with which the kiln is made hot. Afterwards, only small bundles of twigs are used. With these the burning is continued for three or four days and nights; when both the bricks and chalk have somewhat cooled, they are covered over the top with moss or furze blended together, such as they had cut and bound together on the common.

"At the same time all the kiln-mouths are stopped, so that no moisture may draw in. Thereupon, the bricks are first taken out and afterwards the chalk, which chalk is now after burning, much lighter than before. It is then slaked with water, like another unslaked lime, when it falls asunder into a fine white meal or powder, which is the lime with which they here build houses, manure arable fields and meadows, etc."

The remains of our kiln can still be seen . . . if you search, that is, amongst the tons of scrap metal, old sinks, etc., with which this historic link with the past has been bequeathed! From the middle of it once grew a magnificent pussy willow tree. From about 1900 and until the last war children of the village collected branches of this pussy willow to decorate the church on Palm Sunday; alas, a custom no longer practised. On the Hoo, and elsewhere, could be found Quaking grasses, harebells, heather and bee orchids, to name just a few. It was a custom at one time for children to meet on Good Friday at the entrance to the Balk, trekking from there to Pegsdon Hills in search of a beautiful, but elusive, purple flower which grew only on the hills, and would appear to have been some sort of wild orchid. I understand it can still be found on Telegraph Hill during June. Wild flowers could also be found in some of our woods, several of which, incidentally, are named after members of the Sowerby family: Thomas's Plantation, Emily's (in Putteridge Park), and George's Plantation; other wood names being Mushroom Elden, Grubb's Bush, Malden Firs and Lilley Park Wood.

Hills leading up to Lilley Hoo, taken from the side of Baulk Lane. PC

Next to the former Wesleyan Chapel, towards the Lilley Arms, used to stand a row of cottages. It was here that old Granny Bland sold her sweets to village children at one time. After the cottages were pulled down the gardens remained as allotments, and one of them was rented by Freddie Brown, who lived with his wife, Annah, in a row of three cottages that have now disappeared into the house known as "Copperhill". Now the Browns were renowned in the village for two things: firstly, Annah always had her weekly wash on her line by 5 a.m. on a Monday morning, and secondly, she and Freddie had a green parrot, which had been given them by Freddie's brother, "Sham" Brown, a regular soldier, who had taught the parrot to say: "Wake up, Gunner, daylight's come!"

Between the house that used to be occupied by Freddie and Annah, and the row of cottages where resided James Boddy, Dorcus Humphrey, Emma and Jacob Webb and Arthur and Kate Coles, is located Balk Lane which was then, as now, a bridleway leading to the Hoo, and Hoo Farm — in 1919 farmed by a Jabez Cook. In this same year there was a spot of bother with Jabez. It appears that he was letting his cattle as well as his sheep graze on the Hoo. This brought protests from other village farmers, and Jabez later gave an undertaking to graze only sixteen sheep to every twenty acres of land, according, it was alleged, to the custom of the Manor. This is very odd, because in 1768/69 a tenant farmer could graze one sheep

Part of the front of the Victorian Lilley Rectory, demolished in the 1950s.   BO

to every acre of land held — twenty sheep to twenty acres. Why only sixteen?

About the time of the building of St. Peter's Church, the old Rectory was demolished and a much larger one built. The barn and farm buildings, which had remained as relics of the days when Rectors received their tithes in kind, also disappeared. The grounds of the new Rectory were laid out by Matthew Feakes, who arrived in Lilley with Rector Haviland in 1868. A dove house, traditionally dating from King John's reign, remained until 1920; by which time it must have been about seven hundred years old.

The Rectory grounds were often the scene of many cricket and hockey matches. It was here that squire Thomas George Sowerby hit the ground's first and only century. Village treats were held here, too, an annual one being on St. Peter's Day (earlier they had been held at Putteridge Park). The Patronal Festival then was a Red Letter day for village children, for it meant jellies and fruit, cakes and lemonade, games and dancing ... and a half-day from school! All the children went to church first, then to their treat. Practically all the village attended a dance in the evening.

Mrs. Haviland laid the foundation stone of a new school in 1875. For five winters previously the Rector and Mr. Feakes had taught children at a night school held in the Reading Room, which building is better described, perhaps, as a village hall or community centre, for among other activities, it housed a mothers' meeting, a library, a boys' club, Lilley Clothing Club and parish council meetings.

I have been unable to trace the origin of either the Reading Room (long since demolished) or "The Sandpits" ... which is a great pity, for 'I feel sure that the latter was worked in conjunction with "The Lime Kiln".

The road by the school and the former Red Lion and bakehouse was always referred to as Back Street. The houses behind the Red Lion are reputed to be very old, and may well have been in existence before the roadside houses and the Red Lion were built. The story goes that at one time they were stables used by Johann Kellermann. (See Chapter 15.) Before his hermit days he was a keen owner of racehorses which he is reputed to have kept in these stables. Because of the construction of the cottages this could well be true. The kitchens have certainly been added since they were built; the chimneys and gables have evidence of doors sealed over which could have been used for the storage of hay and straw, and the existing stairs, too, could be the original ones to the hay loft. These cottages together with the old post office and shop; the old Red Lion; the bakehouse; a general and confectionery shop and a row of Tudor cottages occupied by Willy Titmuss, "Ebbie" Marlow and

Another view of elm trees and the old 'villagey look' that seems now to have disappeared from many villages. Note, too, that old village people do NOT walk on the footpaths provided! BO

The chestnut palings to the left of this photograph were a village feature at one time. Very few, if any, can be seen now. BO

Lilley Manor Farm, the home of the Sowerby family, who used to own Putteridge Bury Park and mansion. BO

Rueley Dell Road as it used to be. Notice the lack of parked cars, and the different type of houses. BO

Emma Toyer, used to form a cluster of dwellings at Back Street, those at the rear having only the post office yard as access.

A very deep well, backing on to the end house in the lane, served the bakehouse with crystal clear, sparkling water, and had the reputation of being the deepest well in the village, over a hundred feet down. It also served all the cottages and shops from the school to East Street corner. The only other wells in the vicinity being at Harry Trussell's Tudor cottage in the field opposite the school and another at Balk Cottages. One on land just off the Green served the inn and the first four cottages in East Street.

The homes once contained in the box-like area of Back Street were almost a community in themselves. The Red Lion at that time was kept by Arthur Toyer, who was something of a character and full of fun (he later moved to Church Farm).

In those days, competition in growing garden produce was strong and much boasting and leg-pulling between friends took place throughout the village. Walking round viewing the flowers one Saturday evening, Fred Holmes noticed that among the yellow pansies were three flowers of different colours on the same root, one having red and blue patches, one with red edges to the petals and the other with a violet centre. This seemed most strange to him, so he called his wife. After some discussion, Willy Titmuss was called to ascertain whether he had ever seen a plant like this. So it went on, until a circle of people, including Arthur Toyer, Fred Godfrey, from the post office, and Will Keeling, all acknowledged experts, stood debating what was the cause of this phenomena, Fred Holmes maintaining that he possessed a secret formula. Some time later, though, Ted Holmes told his, by-this-time proudly puffed-up father, that he had painted the flowers when no one was about!

Seventy-odd years ago, the things most likely to be seen flying, apart from birds, were balloons. Boys ran long distances if one seemed to be losing height, hoping to see it land. When the first air race from Brooklands was arranged, the course included this area. Planes had changed design a bit from the Wright biplane, being mostly monoplanes, but still were no more than a wooden frame and stretched fabric, with low-powered engines, not very reliable. Quite a number of people spent the night on the Hoo, hoping to see some of them. Most of the early top airmen took part, Graham White and Bill Cody among them, but a number did not get as far as the village and several came down in the district ... causing quite a stir.

On another occasion, a plane landed in a field opposite

Putteridge Bury gates at the top of Beech Hill, having run out of fuel. The be-whiskered pilot, with soft helmet and goggles, eventually obtained a fresh supply, and a few spectators were coerced to hang on to the tail and wing-tips to enable him to rev up the engine to the rate required for take-off. Those hanging on the tail had their hats blown off in the slip-stream, but suffered this gladly, thinking perhaps of the stories they would tell in the Silver Lion that night!

Around this time and up to the 1914-18 war, the then village of Leagrave organised a flower show and sports on a rather grand scale, and when possible engaged an airman and plane to demonstrate flying. If there was no great amount of wind, a very daring act for those days — loop-the-loop — was enacted above the hat factories of Luton, causing as much admiration then as the Red Arrows do today.

Harry Trussell had a trap and Fred Holmes occasionally hired this noble chariot and a rather skittish horse to take the family to the show. Others in the village would walk to Warden Hills in order to see the flying, obtaining quite a good view ... costing nothing — which was even better, perhaps!

When the sight of a flying machine was something quite rare, Fred Holmes bought his son a model airship with a clockwork-driven propeller at the rear. The idea was to hang the thing on a cord, wind it up, when it would then fly round and round in circles, suspended by the cord. It also made quite a loud humming noise.

Son Ted and his pals thought that they might cause a minor sensation in the village by hiding behind a hedge and keep the thing going by winding up the clockwork engine slowly. The spot they chose was in a hedge bordering Trussels' Meadow in front of the old post office. They started the airship going. After a short time, Fred Godfrey the postmaster came to his shop door, cocked an ear and listened for a while.

He then dived back, calling "Ulla, Ulla!" (His daughter's name was Ella). "Come out here, there's one o' they ol' flyin' things 'bout".

After a little while, Ulla went and called out the Lines family, then the Keelings, and eventually had all the folks living roundabout, including the bakehouse staff, standing in a group, gazing up, searching the sky for a glimpse of the blessed machine.

"Bugger me", spluttered old Willy Titmuss. "The snotty thing must be goin' round an' round somewhere!"

At this the boys could no longer contain their laughter. Nearly splitting their sides, the three lads bolted across the meadow followed by much shouting. They tried the trick again behind a wall on the Green, opposite the pub, with not quite the same result ... the news had got around!

Although the village is still basically a rural area, there are so many things once seen and heard that have become only memories: the nightingale, which seemed to be singing all around; the barking of foxes; the strange, haunting song of a nightjar from the fields around the Hoo. And things which have passed away with time from the broad acres of this green valley. Like steam from a kettle, they can never return from whence they came: The call of the ploughman to his horses in a language which only they could understand; the plodding of hooves and the thump-thump of cart-wheel hubs as they trundled down the rutted tracks on iron tyres; the whistle from the engines of the huge steam "ploughing tackle" warning the water carrier of their imminent thirst; the tinkle of sheep bells upon the Hoo, which was once a paradise of birdsong, from the sweetest note to the harshest screech.

Here, a short-grass ride ran right across to Blind Lane, a section of the Icknield Way at Pegsdon Hills, which branches up to Telegraph Hill some way before, with a spinney or small copse on top. Here, according to local lore, there once stood a flag-pole, around which were planted trees marking the spot where stood a "telegraph" device used during the Napoleonic Wars — a tall, timber structure with moveable shutters, the top of which was used to send messages across the country from one high point to another. Beside the tower was a wooden building in which lived the crew, two men at a time working in shifts. Messages were read through a telescope and passed on to the next "telegraph".

According to a family story, one of Ted Holmes' ancestors was a shepherd employed on the Hoo during these times, and his two children would take a meal there for him. When his flock were at the farthest end of the Hoo it meant a long walk, so they would sometimes go by the "telegraph" station and talk to the crew. One day, when paying a visit in this way, they were told, in rather bad taste perhaps, that a message had been received stating that the French were landing. This so frightened the children, a boy and a girl, that they ran all the way home, a distance of about three miles, or so the story goes!

During these times, food was so short that only tradesmen, farmers and the gentry had meat to eat, the common man's family often having to live on bread and turnips, and if he stole to feed his children, as like as not he would be severely punished. To get something different from water, stale bread was toasted black and scraped to form a powder to make something resembling coffee in colour to drink. Some children would look through the windows of the more fortunate — like an ancient and pathetic version of the Bisto Kids — just to catch a glimpse of a meal of meat.

Upon the Hoo, once upon a time, could be seen a great number of blackberry bushes, hawthorn and masses of bracken and gorse bushes; a wide area of Scottish heather, planted there for game cover; every kind of grass and wild flower; beech trees, upon which village lads and lasses carved their names and those of their sweethearts; rabbits and hares, stoats and weasels.

Often, at the start of the Great War, the children would be there to see local volunteers taking part in mock battles, with machine guns made of wood, which made a rattling noise by turning a handle, and rifles using blank cartridges. In the distance, they would hear the school bell ring "Wash", giving them just five minutes to make it to school! Such a place was the common known as "the Hoo".

Later on, as motor cars became more numerous and charabanc parties became popular, the common became the "in" place to visit. Hampstead Heath had nothing on this! The lovely green ride became a wide strip of mud, under water in places. Charabancs, as well as cars, drove right across to the farthest corner against Pegsdon Hills. It was difficult to walk through the heather without stumbling over a courting couple, stopping a cricket ball or disturbing a picnic. Frank Howe, a village shopkeeper, took tent and stall to the Hoo most summer weekends to sell oranges, ice-creams and sweets. He was not alone in this, at a time when every penny counted.

An Italian gentleman with barrel organ and monkey dressed in colourful clothes; a rag-and-bone man with a barrow who gave a paper windmill in exchange for a jam jar; a scissors grinder with an ancient treadle machine; a muffin and crumpet vendor who carried a tray on his head; another Italian gentleman who pushed an ice-cream barrow from Luton, all were regular and welcome visitors to a village that was once renowned far and wide for its beauty; and each, like the Hoo itself, has left a memory that will all too soon be erased with the passing of time.

From about 1860 a village blacksmith was located at what must be one of Lilley's most beautiful old cottages (some of the timbers dating from the fourteenth century, and located next to Lilley House), No. 55 West Street. It was also the village post office, at least until 1849.

This cottage has strong associations with John Bunyan, the Bedford tinker and famous author of "Pilgrim's Progress", the story being that he hid in the cellar. But it is just as likely that he preached in the house, because four houses in Lilley were later registered for worship by Protestant Dissenters, so it is obvious he had sympathisers in the village.

Had Bunyan kept a diary his movements would have been more certain, but it has long been established that Bunyan had an aunt, Alice was her name, who lived in Hitchin, and that he preached at Bendish and Preston, and Lilley lies on a route he could have taken from Bedford.

Bunyan's Aunt Alice was the daughter of Thomas Bunyan, of Elstow. She was buried at St. Mary's churchyard, Hitchin, in 1614. His sister Elizabeth was baptised in the town in 1638. His wife and child are believed to have taken shelter in Hitchin during his imprisonment.

At Kings Walden, four or five miles south of Hitchin, lived Sir Matthew Hale, the judge with whom Bunyan's wife pleaded for his release from prison.

Bunyan himself often visited Hitchin and the vicinity, his meetings nearly always being held at night, in the open air, in barns or farm houses.

At Preston, three miles from Hitchin, there is a big dell in Wain Wood where Bunyan would preach to a large congregation in all weather, dry or wet or even icy cold. At times he had to disguise himself in a smock frock and hold a wagoner's whip.

The cottage in Wain Wood in which Bunyan often rested, still stands after three hundred years and is occupied, the same as the cottage in Lilley and possibly others elsewhere.

Chapter 6

Domestic Issues

With a farm worker (and most village men were such) earning from 12s. 6d. to 15s. a week, such things as a lending library and a clothing club were obviously a necessity. Herbert Titmuss, who I believe I'm right in saying, was one of only two men who at one time worked outside the village, earned £1 a week as a painter and decorator in Luton. With this, perhaps, he could afford a little extra "baccy", which he could obtain for a penny to twopence an ounce. Two popular brands were Anchor Shag at 1½d. an ounce and Honeycut at 2d. His bread, a huge cottage loaf, would cost him around 2½d., sugar from a 1d. to 2d. a pound, a 7lb. jar of jam 1s., beef pieces 3d. and suet 1d.

Once or twice a week, Mrs. Feakes (wife of the illustrious Matthew, the Rector's gardener) stood at a copper at the Rectory ladling out hot soup (provided by Rector and Mrs. Haviland) to those in need, and in the winter months, I am told, there were some who attained, at the best, merely starvation level. It has been said that at this season some local farmers would "set off" some of their men. Understandable, perhaps, but causing a great deal of hardship. The men set off made a habit of following the threshing engines in search of casual work. Thomas Foll, a gentleman in the true sense of the word, who farmed Ward's Farm, made a point of having his corn threshed just a few weeks before Christmas for the sole purpose, it is locally believed, of giving work to those unemployed. At a later date, Rector Genge made a present each Christmas of five hundredweight of coal to the elderly of the village.

An opportunity for adding a shilling or two to the family budget was at acorn time, and you can read later on a description of the first acorn tea, held in Miss Cundall's time, in Lilley. The acorn harvest was the last of the year, and everyone, including children, collected as many as they possibly could and stored them in a cool, dry place until they were collected by the farmers for about one shilling a bushel, to be fed to pigs and sheep.

I dare say, after this harvest, a child would be given a copper or two as reward for hard work. If this is so, there were various ways a penny could be stretched quite a long way. John Boddy could have spent a hard-earned copper by purchasing from Lawrence's general shop a halfpenny-worth of dates; or half a pound of mixed boiled sweets from Granny Bland for three farthings; or a pennyworth of "crinklings" (or "crackling"), the rind off roast pork, from Lizzie Cain.

In 1901 the golden sovereign bought almost seven times as much as its paper counterpart does today. Britain was prosperous. Trade was expanding, but the rising costs of the South African War caused Income Tax to be put up by 2d. to 14d. (preferred by the Treasury to 1s. 2d.). The Chancellor of the Exchequer, Sir Michael Beach-Hicks, said he did not look forward to a permanent Income Tax at 14d. in the £.

Duty on a bottle of whiskey was 1s. 3d. The same liquid cost 16s. 6d. a gallon. Ordinary claret was 11½d. a bottle and champagne started at 3s. 4d. and brandy at 3s. 1d. India pale ale was 2d. 9d. a dozen bottles or Guinness Extra Stout at 13s. 6d. for an eight-gallon cask. Pipe tobacco cost less for a pound than an ounce costs today, and Navy Cut cigarettes were 3s. for a hundred, with Havana cigars from 6d. upwards.

A big joint of beef for the family cost 9d. a lb., York ham 1s. a lb., and Christmas puddings 1s. 1d. a lb. For the children, clockwork train sets with rails started at 2s., toy prams at 10s. 6d. Sweets included bull's eyes, 1s. 1d. for a 2lb. jar and almond rock at 7d. a lb. The usual Saturday pocket money for a child was a halfpenny.

But, as always, there was another side to the picture. Prices were low, but so were wages. Average pay in industry and on the railways was about 25s. a week. A coal miner worked long hours underground for about 4s. 3d. a day, and a housemaid received £15 to £20 a year. A doctor started in a hospital at £2 a week, and in the village a specialist farm workers' wage was about 12s. 6d., perhaps a little more, working from dawn to sunset, six days a week. On this he probably brought up a family of eight or nine or even more.

A popular way to stretch the family budget was by keeping a pig or two. The sow, compared with some humans, in fact lived in comparative luxury, her evening meal being a regular ritual, consisting of fattening ingredients, which prepared her for her execution. This was carried out by "Shaddy" Saunders in the yard behind his house, or by Cain the butcher, for which they received a small remuneration. After her demise, Mrs. Hog was strung up to drain off her blood, prior to being cut into joints of pork or bacon. After this, mother would get to work curing the bacon and pork joints in brine and hanging them up to dry. There would also be an abundance of "chitterlings" and lard. And a sharing of joints of pork with neighbours, of course.

A recognised pig-keeper at the turn of the century was a local worthy called Nottage, head coachman to Rector Haviland, who lived in one of the three thatched cottages in East Street. It was the custom for children, whose parents did not keep pigs, to take to him the Sunday dinner scraps to be manufactured into "swill" for the pigs. For this service, each child received a small sum of money — perhaps a halfpenny; sometimes a penny.

Most of the cottages in Lilley (alas, many of them have now disappeared) were of the four-roomed type; living room and kitchen downstairs and two bedrooms up. When one thinks of the size of families that were in vogue eighty-odd years ago, one wonders how they managed to stay so fit and well in such cramped surroundings. Most of the cottage floors downstairs were of bricks simply pounded into the earth. As we have already seen, cottagers that were able would have coconut matting, but the less fortunate would have sacking; the industrious a rag rug, and water for drinking was got from wells, and what marvellous water it was. Clear as a bell. I can just remember having to draw water from a well in Saunders Yard. Each well probably served a dozen cottages, and the water was stored in large, glazed earthenware pans.

Drains being few and far between, some slops were thrown on the garden, and soapy water over flowers and fruit bushes (which accounts, no doubt, for the absence of any serious pests). There used to be a large gooseberry bush outside Sam and Susan Bland's back door. That bush received more soap than the average child receives in its schooldays, as well as soot and home-made concoctions, but what luscious fruit it bore! And never a trace of disease. A lesson for modern gardening techiques, to be sure.

Childish illnesses were often treated with home concoctions, such as the good old remedy for most ailments, salt and senna, brimstone and treacle. In addition to these, herbs were also greatly believed to have healing properties; and not only herbs, but any plant that could be used for medicinal purposes, were greatly respected, and I have proved from experience that these herbal remedies do indeed work: Stewed groundsel was used for poultices; marshmallow leaves and flowers made into ointment for boils; lily leaves for cuts; dock leaves for galled feet; green broom for the kidneys; dandelion roots for liver troubles; coltsfoot leaves for bronchitis and asthma; rue pills for a tonic; and the leaves of camomile, yarrow and agrimony were used for making herb tea, which was sugared to taste.

So far, we have taken a rather romantic peep at village life. As always, however, there was another side to the picture. In the latter half of 1887 the poor old farmworker was forced to take a cut of one shilling in his meagre weekly wage. It was generally felt by the workers themselves that there was no necessity for this lowering of wages, and many attributed the cut to the farmers trying to take advantage of the "poor" at a slack time of year.

However, to get a fair picture of the agricultural situation existing in 1887, it is necessary for us to go back to the time of the Napoleonic Wars. When the squires and their tenant farmers prospered. The necessity of producing food at home then, without relying to any great extent upon imports, caused much land to be brought into cultivation. The squire received high rents for his farms and the farmer received high prices for his produce, while the farm worker, whose wages were low, received a "dole" from the parish funds to supplement them.

After the return of peace, agriculture fell upon evil days. Much land went out of cultivation and rents fell. An attempt was made to stabilise prices by the passing of the Corn Law of 1815, which prohibited the importation of corn while the market price was below eighty shillings per quarter (480 lb.). It was hoped that this measure would have the effect of stabilising corn prices. If, owing to an abundant harvest, the price of corn fell, imports would cease, and the fall would not go far. If the price rose in times of scarcity, corn would be imported, and the rise would not be great. It was hoped that the price of a quarter of wheat would always be between seventy and ninety shillings, and it was contended that wheat would never be so cheap that it would not pay the farmer to grow it, nor bread so dear that the poor could not afford to buy it. But this infamous law inflicted only the maximum of hardship on the poor of town and country alike — with the price of bread at famine level — without affording the expected relief to farmer and squire. Rents continued to fall, and market prices to fluctuate violently. The position was made worse by the unsatisfactory nature of several of the harvests in the years around 1815. The following year the price of wheat varied between fifty-four shillings and one hundred and seven shillings per quarter. In 1828, the Corn Law was modified, a sliding scale being substituted for the provisions of the Act of 1815, but little improvement was effected.

In 1834, the first step was taken to improve the farmworkers' position. The system of giving doles to supplement wages was ended. For a time this, the poorest class in the country, suffered terribly, since wages were so low that the labourers and their families were perilously near actual starvation. But, however great the suffering entailed upon them by the ending of the doles, it was necessary to take this step in order to rescue these people from the pauperism and degradation involved in the old system. In course of time wages slowly rose.

The repeal of the Corn Law in 1846 was opposed violently by the landed interest in Parliament. The squires saw in this measure the ruin of agriculture. Yet the industry was not ruined, and corn prices fluctuated much less violently during the thirty years following the repeal than in the similar period of the existence of the law.

The earlier half of Victoria's reign was a period of progress and improvement in agriculture, though the industry can be regarded as really prosperous only between 1850 and 1875. Better methods of cultivation were followed. Manures and fertilisers (bonemeal, phosphates, guano) were applied to the land, and machinery was used to a greater extent than hitherto for such operations as ploughing, reaping, sowing and threshing. Harvests were good, and the increase in population maintained the demand for farm products, so that prices remained satisfactory. The establishment of a network of railways facilitated the marketing of agricultural produce and enabled the farmer to obtain his seed, machinery and manures without difficulty.

Towards the close of the nineteenth century, however, English agriculture was again in a desperate condition, due largely, it would seem, to the cultivation of huge tracts of North American prairie land — and the resulting cheap imports of wheat to this country — and diseased animals at home. Many farms went entirely out of cultivation and rents fell steadily, so that landowners had to be satisfied with much reduced incomes. Farmworkers demanded higher wages at a time when farmers alleged they were forced to reduce them, and many young men left the rural areas to live and work in towns.

These then are the facts on a national level. What was the local reaction to this wage cut? An article of the time, written by a local man, comes down pretty heavily on the side of the landowners.

The writer pointed out that turnips were a failure, there was but little hay and clover. Wheat was fetching on an average — and only best wheat was sold — twenty-nine shillings per quarter of eight bushels. Oats averaged fifteen shillings and barley twenty-nine shillings. Profit on stock and sheep was as a rule only on the manure they made. The article made the point that the drop in prices had to benefit somebody. Who was the gainer, the writer asked? The middle man? The butcher? The miller? The baker? Not of necessity.

He pointed out that a rich man probably found much of his capital unemployed. He merely made the same "rate" of profit, which was quite another thing from being the same "amount" of profit. The people who benefited from cheap prices were the consumers, and among them were the very labourers who suffered a cut in wages. My view, however, is that because the landowners were making less profit than hitherto was surely not a moral justification for cutting the wages of their employees, who themselves found life far from easy and most certainly had no money behind them whatever.

To defend his viewpoint, the writer draws an illustration of the purchasing power of money over a three-year period.

He said: "We will suppose a man to have received or spent his wages three years ago (1884) in wheat (or bread) at five shillings a bushel, mutton (or meat) at eightpence per lb. and wool (or clothing) at one shilling and threepence per lb., for these are some of the main things a farmer produces and a farm labourer consumes. Well, the farmer is paying the labourer or the labourer can buy with his wages, the same quantity of bread, meat and clothing today as was the case three years ago, and probably more. In other words, while the purchasing power of produce from the farm has decreased, i.e. while the produce of one acre will not buy so much gold or money as it used to do, the gold which a labourer receives will purchase more of the produce of the acre, even though he receives £26 a year instead of £28.12s."

So there we have it in a nutshell. The employer was making less money; his workers on the other hand, he alleged, were better off because of cheap prices. So they had their wages cut. This meant they were in the same state as before the depression, while employers, saving possibly anything from twleve shillings to twenty-four shillings a week on wages, were also enjoying the cheaper prices which were supposed to benefit the poor.

Most of the farm hands mentioned above had more than likely started off their careers as boys at a farm, undertaking a variety of menial tasks, and earning perhaps a few pence a week. One task they would almost certainly have been set for long hours was bird scaring in the fields with a pair of clappers, an oblong bat to which was bound a square of wood on either side and tied together with a leather thong.

The farm lads having successfully or otherwise kept our feathered friends from devouring the corn seed, the time for cutting came round, a time of aching muscles, touchy tempers, long hours and perhaps a certain amount of envy, as the boys beheld the smooth action, the "unhurried" haste of the men with scythes. The gang of mowers began very early in the morning, rested at mid-day and then continued their mowing until dusk. The leading mower was always referred to as "Lord of the Harvest", Lord in this case meaning the man who set the pace. The aim of mowing was to achieve a level cut, and the closer in line that the ears could be left, the easier it was to tie it into sheaves and the quicker it dried out.

Later, of course, various reaping machines were invented, to be followed eventually by the horse-drawn self-binder, which at first was viewed with a great deal of suspicion by the older farm hands, and perhaps there was some justification for this attitude; after all, it meant the passing of an era that had lasted many, many years, and the disappearance of yet another skill in the cause of mechanisation.

The stubble was cleared by horse-drawn carts and wagons, which are dealt with in the next section. Meanwhile, the farm lads were put to "drag" the stubble with a large wooden rake, or one with iron teeth, which in some areas was called a "hobby rake". This operation was usually followed by the gleaners, who in earlier times perhaps had the grain ground for them at a mill like the one at The Flints.

The farmers' dried and carted corn, for generation upon generation, was threshed by the flail. Most flails were made of a five-feet long rod of ash; a "beater-rod" or "swingle" of ash or some other hard wood was attached, making the whole thing about eight feet in length. The use of the flail was very hard and exacting work, which took place in a large barn — with a specially prepared floor — containing a door at either end to create a through draught, thereby aiding the "winnowing" process — the separating of grain from the husks or whiskers.

Following the flail, came the invention of the threshing drums, powered eventually by the huge traction engine, a feature of farm life that is still remembered by many of us today, for a steam engine attracts children like a magnet, and I can remember watching with awe and wonder, those huge engines first manipulating the village street, then manoeuvring into position in the rickyard of Ralph's Farm; the huge wheel that whirled round the driving belt attached to the drum.

Then followed the ploughing. Ploughing with a pair of horses and a single-furrough plough — often before the arrival of the threshing "tackle" — conjures up a picture of serenity and peace of mind, despite it being hard work. Perhaps it has something to do with the same satisfaction one gets from digging; the realisation, maybe, of a power greater than man; so that alone in a field with the fresh brown earth, the patient horses, the inevitable birds; in the distance a church spire, a straw stack here or hayrick there, an autumn tang in the air, one is completely overcome by the immensity of nature, a feeling that whatever harm man can do; however much he may intrude, seedtime and harvest (even if only in the hedgerow) will always be, as surely as night follows day.

When the Great War had begun, and many of the younger men had left the village to serve their country, farmers found it difficult to get labour. In consequence, boys about twelve years old were allowed to be absent from school to work at farms when needed. Because of this a number of lads had rather spasmodic schooling. Not that they minded, of course!

At haytime, after a certain amount of scythe work to enable the horse to draw the cutter without destroying the boundary area, the grass was cut and left to lay for several days. It was then tossed and turned by men with pitchforks. This was a job which village lads sometimes undertook. A horse-drawn hay turner was designed later.

After the grass had lain a few days in the hot June sun — when the gardens were full of the scent of roses, when the snapdragons and the sweet williams bloomed before the cottage doors, and the bees were busy among the honeysuckle — it was turned again. This continued, according to the weather, until the hay was ready to cart. It was then raked into rows across the meadow by means of a horse-drawn rake — or drag as it was then termed, having long curved tines which carried the hay along and could be raised by means of

A happy profusion of rambling and climbing plants at Church Farm at the time a family called Fellowes lived there. JT

a manually operated lever. These rows, neatly regimented, were then formed into "cocks", again by use of the pitchfork. The cocks were so spaced that the horse and cart could be taken between them, and the hay loaded from both sides.

The carts were fitted, both for hay and corn, with timber made "copses", ladder-type extensions to the front and rear, making it possible to increase the load very considerably. One man rode on the cart and arranged the hay, two others tossing it up to him. Boys had the job of "driving cart". This meant leading the horse from one cock to another. Before allowing any forward movement he would call out loudly "Hold tight", as a warning to the man above, and woe betide him if he failed to do this and the passenger fell down into his load, especially if it was nearly completed!

On stopping, the lad called out "Oh-Gee-Whoa", another warning to the man above. With the load completed, a rope was thrown over from the back, pulled tight and lashed at the front to retain the piled-up hay on the cart. The lads were sometimes allowed to try their skill with the coiled rope. The thing to do, they were told, was to throw the rope over so that the other end landed between Dobbin's ears. No easy task, as one can imagine. The horse and cart were then taken by lead rein to where the stack was being built, and another cart and its attendant would be waiting to receive the next load.

To build a hay stack upright and true required so much skill that only the oldest and most experienced farm hands were allowed to perform this task. If for any reason the stack took a lean later on it was propped up by timbers known locally as "Lawyers".

One of the jobs undertaken by boys at corn harvest was "throwing-in", i.e. gathering the sheaves after cutting by the self-binder. Two boys worked together, taking sheaves from some four rows each side and placing them in groups, ears outwards, numbers varying according to crop, but usually nine or ten. The lads were followed by two men who set the sheaves into "shocks" or "stooks" ready for carting.

The loading and carting was of the same order as at haytime, but the distance involved was usually much longer, especially when the stack was being built at the farm. In some cases the journey was done in relays. At Ward's Farm, the longest haul was from Barn Field at the further end of Ward's Wood, and entailed a relay of three boys driving cart. Another long journey was from Mushrooms, a field beside Mushroom Elders.

The tenant of Ward's Farm had a rather frisky horse which was brought into service for harvest, and on one occasion, when carting from Barn Field to the farm, its antics annoyed one of the lads so much that he treated the horse rather roughly. By the time Dick Bland took over it was on the trot — in spite of a full load. While transferring to Ted Holmes at the field before the farm, the horse began to run, the load swaying crazily from side to side, gathering speed with every wild second, until Ted was taking exceedingly long strides in an effort to overtake the headlong rush of horse, cart and sheaves, all the time shouting "Whoa! Whoa!" which only seemed to hasten the mad rush.

The workers building the rick in the farmyard across the way heard the hullabaloo and ran to close the gate. For one awful moment Ted thought the horse would attempt to jump it, load and all, but it stopped right up against the gate, sweating and streaming, and quite unconcerned at Ted's expletives!

Farm workers took food to work in the fields in a large, rather flat woven basket slung on their shoulders. There was a break for "beaver" at mid-morning and another for tea, beside the main mid-day meal, the farm hands usually gathering under a tree, having first provided nosebags for the horses. According to custom, farmers provided liquid refreshment twice a day, at beaver and teatime, from a specially brewed harvest beer, one of the boys collecting it from the farm in a large stone jar.

After a rick had been built to a height beyond reach of those unloading from the cart, an elevator was brought into use which could be raised to the required height by turning a handle, the sheaves being taken up by a series of forks or bars. The means of operation was by a turntable with a pole which was taken round and round by a horse, plodding along hour after hour. If the horse stopped and the sheaves failed to arrive at the top there was a shout of "Gee-up! Gee-up!". This sometimes caused confusion because the horse hitched to the cart being unloaded took it as a reference to him, and off he went, anxiously chased by a boy.

The most welcome call came at the end of the day, when the boy bringing the last empty cart away from the farm, passed on the word "Last cart". It was then usually late in the day and the way home was often in the dusk of evening, with the sun a ball of fire on the western horizon; the bats flitting here and there, dodging obstacles with uncanny accuracy; the plod of Dobbin, the squeak of wheel hubs in need of grease; the chatter of boys, the joking of men, all part of a rural scene that has gone for ever.

Having written about farm workers' wages, farming practice and customs, let us now read about the situation that existed here at the time of the Enclosure of Land Act of 1769. This Act, designed to improve farming methods, but used by some to hide a great big land fiddle, had a profound effect upon village life, causing loss of livelihood, land and crafts that are, happily, slowly returning.

In 1769, farming practice — here as elsewhere — was governed by the Manor Court. That body dictated when a field (or strip) should be sown, with what crop and when it should lie fallow. In fact, a tenant had no option but to observed the custom of the village in their cultivation, and the man who thought that better results might be obtained by a change of rotation or by the selection of a different date for sowing or reaping was unable to make experiments. The most industrious were at the mercy of the idlest. The weeds which grew on the land of the latter would spread to that of the former.

Changes in agricultural methods had been made from time to time, but they were neither profound nor widespread, and there was opportunity to apply them only on the enclosed farms, leasehold and freehold, which existed here and there. Some manuring was done, some changes in rotation had been made, some new devices had been invented, but these things did not touch the open fields.

In the eighteenth century, the population was increasing, and towards the end of the century the rate of increase was considerable. More food was needed, but the yield could not be enlarged under the old system which, therefore, had to give place to another. Scarcity of food naturally produced a tendency to a rise in prices. The prospect of getting more if he could produce more was likely to make the most old-fashioned farmer overhaul his methods. The great need was for the cutting up of the open fields and re-allocation of the land among the people in consolidated blocks which might be enclosed. Canon Francis Aidan Hibbert, Rector of Lilley in the early 1920's, however, tells us what really happened:

"In 1769, the Lord of the Manor here was Sir Benjamin Rawling. Sir Fitzwilliam Barrington, of Offley, owned much of the land, and others who owned a good deal were Eleanor Percy, Henry Weston and Thomas Stokes. A petition was sent from these to Parliament that the 951 acres of common land might be redistributed. Hexton had been dealt with three years previously. Of course, there was no opposition here for the ordinary people probably knew nothing about it, and the order was made for the common lands to be redistributed and enclosed. The Rev. Thomas Whitehurst, of Hitchin, William Freeman, from Leicestershire, and John Willis, of Offley Hoo, were appointed Commissioners. The land was viewed by two farmers from Barton and Higham Gobion, and in the final award it is stated that public meetings were held to discuss the business.

"Everybody concerned had to set forth his claims, and then the Commissioners drew up their scheme of re-arrangement. The Manor Estate had long ago been let out to farmers and was not dealt with. Ten people owned a few acres each in the common fields as well as their cottages and gardens. These were John Young, Richard Dawes, Edward Samm, William Dawes, Ann Crouch, John Trussell, Ralph How, Elizabeth Tarryer, Isaac Field and Hannah Cain. Seven people had just a cottage and a garden. All had grazing rights in the common fields. The 951 acres were re-arranged into compact blocks. There is no record of the previous holdings of the smaller landowners but how they were treated may be judged from the Rector's treatment. For his 68 scattered acres he received 21 acres in Sour Hill Field. The seven smallest people were given an acre each in Haredell Field. The others received a few acres each there. The churchwardens had to exchange their two acres, nine poles there which the Lord of the Manor wanted, for one acre, two roods, 23 poles further north.

"The Highway Surveyors were awarded about two acres, and it was stipulated that certain roads were to be kept up. The old Icknield Way was to be 60 feet wide, and footpaths were set out in detail.

"The roads were to be kept in repair by the owners of land which adjoined them. This left the main part to be divided among the big people. Sir Fitzwilliam Barrington received the lion's share — 100 acres in West Field, 107 elsewhere, in addition to 107 acres in East Field. He received about a third of the whole. In lieu of his rights of pasturing a cow on the highways and balks, he was given 12 acres in Coplow Field, which may be contrasted with the eight acres which were divided among the seven cottagers who each claimed a similar right. Henry Weston received 114 acres in Wards Wood Field and the West Field, 30 acres in East Field, 36 acres on Mouse Hill, etc. Eleanor Percy received about the same amount.

"The cost was £765 and was divided among the people concerned, except that the Rector and those who received less than six acres each were excused payment. So the payments ranged from Barrington's £263 to John Trussell's £4. The money was collected by Lawrence Times of Hitchin.

"It was, of course, inevitable that the big people should get their full share, because they could make the most of their claims, while the lesser people would often have difficulty in setting out their claims at all.

"Many of them could not read, and none of them had any experience of legal matters. They had no deeds to produce; all they could say was that as long as they could remember they had kept a cow on the common lands and turned loose their poultry there, and pulled firewood out of the brushwood, as their fathers had done before them." So says Hibbert.

It is easy to see that the one acre received by some people was of no earthly use to them, and so they sold it to those who already had too much. The country crafts slowly disappeared, people began to wander to the towns in search of work, and country life received its first big upheaval.

Chapter 7

Some Entertainment

Harvest homes were an important part of village life many years ago. They were held by custom in a barn at Manor Farm. Village people enjoyed singing and dancing, beer and minerals . . . and piles of food. Music was supplied by local men.

Concerts, too, were a regular feature of life here about the time of the First World War and just after. In 1892 they were something of a rarety, so when Rector Haviland organised one on April 19, 1892, we can guess it was very well attended. It was held in the school, and was for the benefit of the village cricket club. Mr. Haviland was in the chair.

In a diary kept by Miss Dora Haviland at the time we read:

> There were daily practises of the Toy Symphony from April 7, Miss Lilian and Miss Violet Sowerby playing violins. April 14: Lilian, Dolly and Violet came down at 3.30 and we practised before and after tea. It is not at all perfect yet. There was difficulty with the C trumpet which had to be made in tune with stamp paper. The G trumpet is out of tune unless blown in a certain way. Aimee does the nightingale very nicely. They were all excused their lesson with Miss Cundall as the practise is very important. April 19 (the day of the concert): Practised in the school directly after breakfast. One hundred chairs were arranged in rows and a few benches behind. A red cord divided shilling from sixpenny seats. Went down to the school at 6.30 and waited in classroom till 7. Room was very crammed, men at the bottom could hardly move their hands to clap, but they behaved very well. Threepenny people had very little room. Symphony first, then songs. Everything a great success. Alec sang three songs, Lady Ellen four.

The complete programme was:

1 Robberg's Toy Symphony, the Misses Sowerby, the Misses Haviland and Masters W. and L. Haviland; 2 Song, "The Gift", Lady Ellen Lambart; 3 Song, "Off to Philadelphia", Mr. A.K. Gordon; 4 Piano solo, Miss Eleanor Haviland; 5 Song, "Douglas Gordon", Miss Sowerby; 6 Song, duet, A.K. Gordon and Miss E. Haviland; 7 Duet, "Venetian Song", Lady Ellen Lambart and Miss Sowerby; 8 Piano solo, Miss Katharine Haviland; 9 Song, "The Yeoman's Wedding", Mr. A.K. Gordon; 10 Song, "A Bunch of Cowslips", Lady Ellen Lambart; 11 Duet, March (by Beethoven), Miss Eleanor Haviland, Miss Katharine Haviland; 12 Song, with guitar, Miss Sowerby; 13 Song and chorus, "Silver Threads Among The Gold", Mrs. Haviland and children.

Sixty or seventy years ago, I cannot quite determine when exactly, villagers were enlivened once a week by the visit of an Italian gentleman from Luton with a barrel organ. I wonder if he was accompanied by the traditional monkey? About the same time, dancing outside the Lilley Arms to a fiddler was greatly enjoyed, and an annual event in which most of the village children took part was dancing round the Maypole, a delightful custom which takes place only at a few places now.

I have deliberately refrained from mentioning "The Green" in connection with these events because, contrary to local opinion, the village does not possess much of a Green . . . though I suspect that at one time the small parcel of ground, which is now called 'The Green', was much larger than now.

The whole area round here was, in Medieval times, and up to 1768/69, part of a huge area of "waste" which lay around and beyond Lilley Park Wood. In the Enclosure of Land Act of 1768 most of this "waste" was distributed and fenced, except, I submit, the ground we call "The Green", which has remained as waste ever since; even though it has been registered as common land.

The meadow next to the Lilley Arms, at one time belonging to the inn, was the scene of a village fair, held twice a year for three days. Called Bland's Fair, it boasted the usual stalls, roundabouts, swinging boats and barrel organ. To add to the merriment, village lads could purchase tubes filled with water to squirt at each other, which they did with great gusto.

On most Saturday evenings dances were held in the Victory Hall (so called to celebrate the Armistace of 1918), often attended by between eighty and ninety people. Usually the Master of Ceremonies was Frank Howe and the Folkes' brothers played the piano.

Also held in the Victory Hall was a regular concert, exploiting local talent, of which there appeared to be a surfeit. At these village concerts, Jim Allingham and Freddie Farr were two popular comedians. One can imagine, too, that Dick Bland and Ted Holmes had something to say at these events. It appears that our Rectors usually acted as chairmen.

On a summer Sunday evening, after church, the young people of Lilley would walk towards Offley, and those of Offley towards Lilley, the two parties meeting 'twixt the two. There is no evidence of what went on at these meetings, but young people are young people whatever their generation!

The annual choir outing by train to Yarmouth was an occasion for much merriment. To make the journey more interesting the menfolk reckoned to drink a pint every time they saw a windmill. I suspect that after a few pints many more windmills were seen than actually existed!

Once a year Rector Haviland would invite choirboys, men, bellringers and their wives to the Rectory for a slap-up meal. Afterwards, each choirboy had a choice of either a pair of boots, a suit or an overcoat, according to his need.

Most of us at some time or other have heard from our great-grandparents about the celebrations in the village on St. Peter's Day, when Lilley really used to go to town for its patronal festival; a day that was, no doubt, as important then as our annual holiday is now.

Some years later things had died down a bit. On July 1, 1904, the children of the school wrote a letter to Miss Dora Haviland (whose family by this time had left the village) describing a St. Peter's Day that took place then. It said:

> Dear Miss Haviland, On St. Peter's Day we went to church at half-past-two and we sang, "We Love The Place O God" and "The Son Of God Goes Forth To War". Mr. Genge preached the sermon and Mr. Arthur Foll played the organ. Before we went into church we all walked round the grave (of Rector Haviland – Author). It looks so nice, for many roses are in bloom. There was a large

wreath, and two anchors and a cross full of flowers. We school children took a very large wreath of dog daisies, " In loving remembrance".

After the service the infants and old people rode up to Putteridge in the vans. Old Mrs. Webb from the Almshouses went and so did Mary Anne Thompson and Patience Cain. Old Mrs. Bland was not well enough to go. Our mothers walked. There was someone from every house in Lilley. After the service we walked through the Park carrying flags.

We saw a great many little pheasants, some wild ducks, a skylark on her nest and five scarecrows as large as men and women. We reached the lawn just as the clock struck four. Major and Mrs. Sowerby met us. The infants were there before us, so after saying grace, we began tea under the beautiful large trees.

We were very warm, but it was quite lovely in the shade. We had tea, bread and butter and two kinds of cake. Mrs. Gerald Bodsworth and Lilian Bland's mother cut the bread and buttered it. Mr. Genge was there, but he soon went away after tea to catch the train.

After tea we went where we liked and some of us went over the house. The younger children had toys from a bran tub and we ran for prizes. The boys had some three-legged races and potato races. There were some nice swings.

The eagle is dead, but we saw a stuffed eagle. We saw a fountain and a sundial. After spending a very pleasant day we sang "God Save The King". Mr. Feakes thanked Mr. and Mrs. Sowerby and with some hearty cheers we left soon after eight o'clock.

Will you please accept some daisies from the hayfield. Governess says when Mr. Edmund comes to London you are coming to see us and it makes us glad. We wished you lived at the Rectory. We remain, yours lovingly, The Children of Lilley School. No one went from Mrs. Cook's house because they were not well enough.

Ten or so years after the above event took place Bank Holidays were an excuse for a male tour of local inns. In the village, outside the Lilley Arms on one such Bank Holiday, the late Bob Titmuss was, well, a little the worse for drink. A few of the village lads "borrowed" a donkey from Jabez Cain, placed Bob on the animal facing its rear, tied his legs beneath its belly, and gave the donkey an almighty whack. The result, I am assured, was hilarious!

Bob Titmuss lived here. He was a wood cutter and swept chimneys – a real village character. BO

It was August 3, 1867. William Bradbury, of Lilley, wanted new clothing. He decided to walk to Luton to buy some. He delayed his return until the public houses opened. He had money to spend; he was going to enjoy himself. He reached Round Green as the midnight hour struck. He was to go no further.

William Worsley, Levi Welch and James Day, all of Luton, had been drinking at the Jolly Topers. All three left together and walked a short distance towards Stopsley. Day dropped a sixpence. He fumbled on the ground for it, but could not locate it. He could not afford to lose a sixpence, so he went back to the Jolly Topers to get a light. Worsley and Welch became impatient as Day continued to search, and went on, falling in with Bradbury, meanwhile.

This unfortunate man was found a little later lying in the road bleeding profusely from the head and unconscious, with his pockets cut out. He never regained consciousness, and died shortly afterwards.

Levi Welch acknowledged robbing Bradbury, but, according to the "Bedfordshire Mercury" of March 31, 1868, "positively asserted that he committed no violence upon the person, and that Worsley was the man who felled him to the ground with a heavy grate winch, afterwards kicking him, jolting his head on the ground, and directing how he was to be robbed. Worsley denied this, and adhered to his denial up to the time of his trial. But Welch repeated his confession in Bedford Gaol before the Governor, and frankly owned to his share of the guilt".

The three men were arrested. Day was released. Worsley and Welch stood trial at the Lent Assizes at Bedford on March 16, 1868. Welch was convicted and sentenced to fourteen years' penal servitude. Worsley was sentenced to death, the date for his execution being fixed for March 31, a Tuesday. The Governor conveyed the information to Worsley on Tuesday, March 17, the day after the trial. Worsley replied, "Oh, very well, sir".

The "Mercury" continues: "He has behaved himself becomingly towards the officials of the Prison, one of whom was in constant attendance upon him day and night, and listened attentively to the overtures of the chaplain (the Rev. George Maclear) after his trial. On Saturday, one of his brothers had an interview with the Governor, and during the whole of the day remained in the town making exertions on the prisoner's behalf".

The day before his execution, William Worsley made a statement to the Governor:

"Dear Brothers and Sisters, — I have made a true statement to the Chaplain and Governor, who has taken it down in writing — how this sad affair has happened, and what made me do it, and it is my wish that what I have said may be made known to you, in the hope that it may be satisfactory to you. I never meant to leave this world before I made it known as soon as I found there was no hopes for me. I hope you will forgive me for what I have done. I am quite satisfied with the judge who tried me — also with my counsellor as far as he had information given him. I have only now to thank you all sincerely and the public at large for what you and they have done for me, and hope that the Lord will reward you and them for it.

"I must now bid you all farewell, and pray that this may be a warning to all of you. Give my kind love to my wife, and I hope she will make herself as comfortable as she can about me, and hope she will pray earnestly to the Almighty for guidance and strength during the remainder of her days. I pray now day and night for the merciful God to forgive me, and I hope that I shall make my peace with Him ..."

There follows a description of the execution, the last public one at Bedford, which does not make pleasant reading, and is best left in the dim past.

Some time later the "Bedford Town and Townsmen" for 1868 published a sequel to this whole unhappy affair:

"The Last Public Execution. At the March Assizes, William Worsley and Levi Welch were tried for the murder of William Bradbury of Luton. Welch turned approver against his comrade in crime and was acquitted of the capital charge. Worsley was convicted and hanged at Bedford Gaol on March 31st. Welch, who evidently thought he was going to escape, was arraigned for the robbing of the deceased man, Bradbury, and pleaded guilty. He was at once sentenced to fourteen years' penal servitude, to the great satisfaction of all in court. However, in the following July, Welch returned to his home at Luton with a free pardon in his pocket. It seems that a free pardon had been offered to any person not having actually committed the crime, who should give information that would lead to the conviction of the murderer, and as Welch happened to be the informant he was entitled to the fulfilment of the promise."

The inn has always been an integral part of the English way of life, no less in the heart of the countryside than in the centre of an important town, but, nonetheless, a village pub was a very different place at the turn of the century from what it has become today, relying now to a large extent on passing "trade" for its livelihood. Most of the customers long ago were village people . . . who had their own seats in the taproom.

When Harry Taylor took over the Silver Lion about 1904 it

consisted of a large taproom, the bar, a small bar (the jug and bottle), another room used for club meetings and a kitchen. A long passage ran the length of the building. Upstairs were five bedrooms and down below a large cellar. The house was open from an early hour to ten o'clock at night. On Hitchin Market days, drovers called in while their animals milled about outside. Not many women went inside a pub, but a few went to the "little bar" to get beer in a bottle or a jug.

Drinks were less varied then than now. Mild and bitter and stout and porter were the long drinks, whiskey, gin, rum, brandy and peppermint the short drinks. Non-alcoholic ginger wine, lemonade, ginger-beer and ginger-ale were for women and children. Port and sherry were also sold. Beer was 2d. a pint, bitter 3d., porter 2d., whiskey, gin, etc. 2d. a single, brandy 4d., port and sherry 3d. In those days, lemonade, ginger-beer and ginger-ale were put into bottles with a marble in them. The bottle was so shaped that the marble could be forced into the neck and kept in position by a rubber ring. A gadget like a small wooden cup with a stalk inside was used to open the bottle. It was placed over the bottle, tapped smartly, and the marble was pushed down. Later on, more soft drinks appeared, usually in bottles with "push-off" tops. Tobacco and cigarettes sold at the Silver Lion were Wills Honeycut and Shag, 1½d. half an ounce; Goldflake and Woodbines, costing 1d. or 2d. a packet, and Players 2½d. for ten.

Weekends were usually lively affairs with plenty of chatter and laughter. Bad behaviour was not tolerated and anyone getting disorderly was soon put out. When buses began to run along the A505, many people from surrounding villages came out to have a drink and a rest and business was brisk. Quite a number of families sat outside on forms, some perhaps reflecting upon the statue of a rampant lion that guards the southern approach to the village aloft a huge pillar of oak.

Not many landlords were able to make a living from a pub by itself, despite the large contingent of regulars, so Harry Taylor had several other irons in the fire. He was a skilled carpenter, undertaking many jobs around the village, kept one or two horses, and was a carrier, also possessing a governess cart and a float. A large wagon with a covered top was used when he was a carrier. It held about twelve people. The wagon was put up at the Horse and Jockey in Luton (now demolished) while the womenfolk did their shopping.

Renting and cultivating a four-acre field rented from the church also helped to supplement the family income. Harry's daughter was often pressed into service to lead the horse when "setting a furrough", that is to walk up the field with her eyes glued to a white marker in the distant hedge, and to be told when she got there: "Couldn't you do better than that?" as father and daughter gazed at the erratic course she had vainly hoped was straight. Actually, this operation of setting a furrough was a very important function, for it determined the straightness or otherwise of the succeeding furroughs, and to the old-time ploughman that was a matter of some pride! During the First World War the whole family helped when mangold wurzels were the crop. At this time also the pub orchard was ploughed up and many sorts of vegetables were grown and sold at Luton.

Harry, as if he hadn't enough to do, also kept pigs. After being fattened, they were sold at Hitchin Market. But occasionally Arthur Young, the village butcher, killed a pig for the family, the custom being then that he had half and the owner had half. Most of the pigs at the Silver Lion had names. One, for some obscure reason, was called Tryphena, and regulars in the taproom must have wondered what sort of exotic food was devoured at the pub when, in answer to his wife's query, Harry would say: "We'll have a meal off Tryphena today".

Like many other public houses, the Silver Lion ran a "slate club". The menfolk paid a certain sum to the landlord each week, and if they were ill could draw out so much money for a stated period. Then at Christmas came the Slate Club supper. This caused a great upheaval at the Silver Lion. The kitchen was cleared for action, another stove was brought in, huge joints were cooked, piles of vegetables were prepared: potatoes, carrots, brussels sprouts, etc. Huge apple pies filled the house with the scent of cloves, and all was bustle and confusion. Several family aunts helped the Taylors, and long tables were arranged in the taproom and club room. The village butcher and Lizzie Cain did the carving, the others serving at table. It was a lively occasion, and after supper came the entertainment. Harry Trussell could "vamp" on the piano and various people sang their own particular song. Grandfather Bean's speciality was "The Mistletoe Bough", and a peculiar character from The Flints called "Hanger" sang "Three cheers for the Red, White and Blue". There was much laughter, banter and joking.

In fact, practical jokes, funny incidents and entertainment seemed to have played a large part in village life around the time of the Great War.

At one time there were three inns in the village. One could get a nip of whisky for 2d. at the Silver Lion, a pint of beer brewed by the Lucas family of Hitchin at the Lilley Arms, or a pint of Page's Best Ale at the Red Lion.

In 1848 the Silver Lion was part of a row of cottages. The Red Lion, now a private house, has an Abstract of Title dated 1844, which can be seen in the County Record Office. At one time Vestry meetings invariably adjourned to either the Lilley Arms or the Red Lion. The earliest entry I can find concerning this inn was one for 1814 in a vestry minute book. The Red Lion unfortunately closed as a public house round about 1940 . . . because of economics, I fancy.

The last licensee was Laban Lines. A grand-daughter of his writes:

> My grandparents, Mr. and Mrs. Laban Lines, came to live in Lilley about 1905. My grandfather had just retired from the Metropolitan Police and took over the Red Lion public house until its closure. He also farmed the fields going up to the Hoo, and kept pigs, chickens, horses and a cow in the large meadow belonging to the "house". Excess milk and home-made butter were sold to the neighbours. I remember watching my aunt turning the handle of a heavy wooden churn for hours, and the large pans of milk standing in the cellar among the beer barrels. In later life my grandfather became crippled with rheumathoid arthritis, brought on, it was said, by shock when one of the "regulars" fell down the cellar steps and was killed.

The victim of this unfortunate accident was one Joe Clark. It is said he left the bar to go to the lavatory, opened the cellar door, slipped, and fell headlong down the stone steps.

The Lilley Arms, alias the Sugar Loaf, alias the Sowerby Arms has the honour of being Lilley's oldest inn, dating from 1705. The licensee in 1787 was Thomas Conisbee, a member of a family that was always to the fore in village life. In 1852 its name was changed to the Sowerby Arms, and the licensee was John Stormer, who in 1873 was elected as an overseer of the poor. At this time it was a hotel, and advertised itself as possessing thirteen acres of ground.

Its name was changed once more during the Great War, this time to the Lilley Arms. It became known as "The Middl'un" — the middle one — not "The Midland" as some people believe, although the meadow next to the inn was commonly called "Midland Meadow", sometimes "Lilley Arms Meadow".

The ownership of all three inns passed in 1907 from Thomas George Sowerby to T.M. Clutterbuck, of Edgware, brewer; in 1928, from Clutterbuck to Putteridge Estate Co.; and in 1940, from Putteridge to Wells and Winch.

At the beginning of the war horses were being requisitioned for army service. Two local men decided it would be a good lark and a bit of devilment if they did something about it. So one weekend, they set out masquerading as Government officials on horse inspection. They visited numbers of estates and large farms inspecting horses and marking some, which they stated should be got ready for collection in about a day's time. They also visited numerous pubs pretending to be plainclothes officers looking for deserters, and thereby obtained free drinks. No one asked for any credentials!

George Allen was the first village youth to own a motorcycle; something of a hybrid machine about 1922, single gear, belt drive, push and jump start. He lived in a cottage at the Sowerby Avenue gate to Putteridge Bury. Sowerby Avenue then was a narrow, rough road from Stopsley, boasting only a farm opposite Cannon Lane, and with high hedges each side. George set off one morning to go to work at a Luton factory. The machine refused to start. He ran and pushed for a long way and wearing a heavy leather coat, began to feel exhausted, when suddenly the machine fired into life. Before he could jump into the saddle, his coat was caught in the bottom of the machine belt. This wound him down tightly on to the bike. So tightly. in fact, that he could not get his hands to his pockets for a knife to release himself. He had to lay there for about half an hour before a cart came along from the Park and the driver let him loose.

On another occasion, wearing the same leather coat while on his motor-cycle, he was following a lorry up to Round Green. At this time, there was only one road to Stockingstone in front of The Jolly Topers. The lorry was designed to have a canvas top and had hooks along each side. George was rather close to the rear of the vehicle when, with no indication, it turned into Stockingstone Road right in front of George. He turned sharply with the lorry to avoid a crash. To his dismay, however, he found that his leather coat had become hooked to the lorry by the shoulder. He was lifted off his machine and carried along with the bike skidding along under him. His coat gave way and he was dropped right on to his machine, while the lorry carried on, the driver possibly quite unaware of the incident!

Concerts and plays were very much in vogue fifty-odd years ago. One playlet which Ted Holmes remembers included a policeman and a sailor. Ken Boddy had the part of the policeman, being great as any character, able to alter face and voice at will. Dick Bland played the sailor, and both obtained authentic uniforms.

On dress rehearsal night, Ted went to call for Ken. "There's plenty of time", said Ken, looking very much a cop, with a small moustache and a few lines to alter his face. "We'll have a bit of fun."

While Ted stood back in the dark, Ken knocked on his

neighbour's door. "I'm on an investigation", said he to old Sam Brown. "I believe you have a dog?" "Yea", replied old Sam, in a very dubious voice. "Then, sir, could I see your licence?" Unfortunately, the licence had expired. Ken took name and address in a notebook, leaving behind a rather worried Sam, who had not recognised the lad next door.

From there, the two went to a Boys' Club in the Reading Room, from which building some rather "blue" language could be heard through the open skylight. In went Ken and knocked on the door, opened eventually by Tom Little, he being in charge that night. Tom looked startled when Ken walked in and read the riot act to all and sundry regarding the language and left again unrecognised. Ted entered a few mintues later and was told of "the bugger of a new copper" and what had taken place.

Ken then called on an old aunt and sat talking to her about her pension for about five minutes, then went to the Village Hut, where the rehearsal was due to take place. He stood at the entrance to the road as Dick Bland came along, dressed as a sailor. In an officious tone of voice Ken asked for his identification or pass. Dick, of course, could not produce anything, whereupon he was "booked" and warned about wearing the King's uniform. This upset Dick's evening greatly until Ken arrived on the stage for his part, when the hoax was revealed.

On one occasion, at a fete in the Rectory grounds, Harry Brown invented an aerial ride by fixing one end of a steel cable way up a fir tree at the entrance to the Paddock, with a small platform below it on the cable, which stretched about one-third of the paddock's length. To a stake in the ground was a pulley wheel on which was suspended a short cable with a tee-shaped handle. To add to the fun there was no safety net! The ride consisted of hanging on to the "tee" handle and launching oneself off in space and down the cable to the ground. Dennis Darby, who had only one arm, decided to give the ride a try, but found that after launching, he was unable to hold on with one hand. Amid some trepidation he fell to the ground. Fortunately, apart from a few bruises, only his male ego was damaged!

Rather ironically, perhaps, Ken Boddy was later to become a member of the Metropolitan Police. Perhaps his earlier impersonations of the "law" served some useful purpose after all. If Dick Bland were still alive, no doubt this book would have run to several volumes such were his many anecdotes.

Former village May Day celebrations did not include a May Queen or Maypole dancing. This latter was kept for St. Peter's Day. Practice took place in the school playground over a period of time before June 29. The Maypole was fitted into a heavy wooden, weighted base. John Boddy many times provided music sitting on the base, with a melodion or sometimes a mouth organ. His usual tune was "The Keel Row".

Children gathered May and other flowers or blossom to go "Maying", but their visits were limited. School governess Esther Cundall, though, was a must. Outside her door they sang part of an old Hertfordshire Maying song, which perhaps did not set too cheerful a note with which to welcome spring:

Remember us, for May is here, and now we do begin,
To lead a life of righteousness or else we die in sin.
To die, to die, to die in sin, what a dreadful thing
t'would be,
For our poor souls would always lie in pain and misery.
Repent, repent, ye wicked, wicked men, repent while ye
are here.
For when you're dead and in your grave, there's no
repentance there.
This sprig of May to you I bring, and at your door
I stand,
It is but a sprout, but well budded out, and the
work of our dear Lord's hand.

On Easter Day, the Sunday School class under Esther Cundall, after assembly at school, attended morning service. Afterwards each received an Easter Egg.

Every year there was a party, or school treat as it was called, nearer Christmas. Each child was asked about a week before what they would like as a present, and as far as possible received it at the treat. These things, for a time, were provided by Mrs Clutterbuck, of Putteridge Bury.

She did a lot for children of the school, providing dinners for those who could not get home or were too poor . . . in her opinion, at least, for people of this era were a proud lot. I can remember my grandmother telling a tradesman at the door she had no change. What she should have said was she had no money!

The meals arrived in a specially made wooden container, with insulation provided by a layer of hay which was pressed between an inner and outer box, the lid was also double and insulated in the same way. The whole thing was very heavy and took two boys all their time to carry it into school, but the soup and food were still pretty hot, although having come by pony and trap all the way from the mansion.

Mrs Clutterbuck also gave magic lantern entertainment to children and parents, with coloured slides of her visits to India and her tiger hunting there. She was proud to show a tiger rug made from a skin taken from an animal shot on safari. And also a picture of herself riding an elephant.

Another of her good deeds was in providing wooden clogs for school children to keep their feet dry in bad weather . . . much to the disgust of Johnny "Snob" Sansom, who hated mending the "bloody" things!

A favourite activity with village lads was "bird folding", which took place at dusk. Equipment was a net fixed between two long sticks or light poles. This was carried by boys one side of a hedge, with others shining bright lights, while on the other side their pals would beat the hedge. The birds taking roost, frightened out of their lives, would fly out and into the net which was then folded. This may seem unnecessarily cruel, but one should remember that money was short and sparrows and blackbirds were reputed to be quite succulent when prepared for table.

A mischievous pastime was "pin and button", which meant hanging a button, suspended on a short piece of cotton tied to a pin, stuck above someone's window with another length of cotton tied to this, thereby enabling the participants to tap the window while being well hidden some distance away. A Mr Ebsworth, who lived in a large house near the church, was a fairly regular victim. The knocker on his front door was also used by tying cotton to it. He would come to the door, look around and seeing no one, go in and shut the door again. After a short pause, another knock, followed by another opening, but this time with a lantern. A quick look around, an annoyed grunt and in again. This performance was repeated until eventually the poor man discovered the cotton; but by this time the "birds had flown".

Apple "scrumping" was a regular autumn event. Farmer Arthur Toyer, unfortunately for him, had an orchard some two hundred yards from his farm at Rueley Dell, and this was often raided. Micky Goodge, that prime minister of mischief, was usually there. He would suggest, sometimes, that he and his pals go to the lime kiln to catch rabbits, but Arthur Toyer seemed to have an intuition of this intention and would often turn up and chase the lads off. His foresight gained for him, perhaps a little unkindly, the title of "Forty Foxes".

He was successful once in catching Micky. It happened like this: Having grown some very nice tomatoes at the side of the pond wall inside the farmyard approach, he was rightly proud of his prowess. Micky, together with Ken Boddy, Dick Bland and some others, decided to take a few. The farm gate was closed for the evening so they climbed quietly over and, when about to help themselves, Arthur Toyer came rushing out of the farmhouse door with a hammer in his hand. Everyone bolted for the gate and clambered over . . . all except Micky that is. He unfortunately got caught up by his trousers on the pointed palings, and in that helpless state received a good belting from a gleeful and very satisfied farmer.

During the first war, a tented camp was established at Whitehill Farm for a time, with a large number of mules and transport vehicles. To amuse themselves in off-duty time, some of the troops built a model village in a shallow dell alongside the camp to the right of the footpath to Whitehill beyond Ward's Wood. At Warden Hills there was a firing range with sentries posted at various places to warn people it was dangerous to proceed beyond that point because of bullets which, often hitting the back of the range, would ricochet a long distance in all directions. Needless to say, several local lads found quite a number in gate posts and tree trunks. One of the sentries patrolled along the edge of a field beyond the wood. Boys would go along and talk to him, and on several occasions Micky managed to "swipe" a round or two of ammo.

He took a bullet home one day. To see what the result would be he threw it in the fire. Fortunately, no serious damage from the resultant explosion occurred, beyond a smashed mirror and a much-chastised Micky! Ted Webb also "obtained" some bullets. He, too, threw one in a fire . . . and blew up the fireplace! Another lad, not to be outdone, obtained some live ammunition. and as an experiment took out the bullet, fixed the case in Jim Boddy's work vice, and hit the cap with a hammer — with noisy and startling results: The work bench shook, the tools jumped, rats ran for their lives, mice disappeared down holes, and the two pals hid themselves with much haste!

When carbide gas vehicle lamps were in use, a school inspector used to ride a motor-cycle to the village and empty a container on the grass bank outside the school. Ted Holmes and his pals sorted out any pieces of carbide not completely used and, together with any they could scrounge from other sources, placed them in a tin. Screw-top bottles were then procured. Into the bottles would go some pieces of carbide and then a little water, thus creating a gas. The cap was screwed on, the bottle stood up, while Ted and Co. retired a suitable distance away to await the result — usually a loud bang and flying glass. If this did not happen, they would pelt the bottle with stones and the first hit usually did the trick.

During the Great War, the Royal Engineers often laid telephone cables along hedgerows about the village from a big drum on a horse-drawn carrier. Ted and Co. made this operation a game by obtaining some Tagell, a cord-like hat material, of which there was plenty, from anyone who had some to spare. They made a truck complete with reel and would "lay cable" along the hedgerows. Incidentally, this material made good boot laces! The lads later discovered that by stringing one end to the bottom of a can, taking it up the tree which stood beside Doozley Pond, and stretching the Tagell across the meadow to an elm tree beside Trussell's shed, they could send coded messages to each other by tapping the tins.

In the village's inns, dominoes was the main pastime. "Running out", "fives-and-threes" and "putt" being the most popular forms.

Sometimes, if enough were interested, "Tip-It" was played using the taproom table, two teams sitting each side. A coin was used, and the game started by the captain of one side tapping the coin on the table, and then with it in his hand take it below the edge, where all the rest of his team had their hands, and pass the coin along, or perhaps still hold it himself. After a brief space of time, he would say "up" and all of his team would place their clenched fists on the table. No. 1 of the opposing team would then, after looking along the line of fists, choose one and say either "take it away" or "tip it", usually the former. If the coin was not in the hand when he said "take it away", the hand was removed, and so on. If he said "Take it away" and the hand held the coin, then that game was lost and a certain number of points went to the opponents. If one side retained the coin for five consecutive sessions, then the next one had to be done above the table and not out of sight.

Another popular game was called "The Devil among the Tailors" on a sloping topped table. A spinning-top was spun by a cord at the top and guided down to a set of nine small pins set rather like nine-pins, the idea being to floor as many as possible while the top was still spinning.

At the Sowerby Arms, there was played "Ring the Bull". In the right-hand corner of the bar, just below the ceiling, was a replica of a bull's head, with its two horns. Suspended from the ceiling about halfway across the room was a ring about six to eight inches in diameter. The game was to swing the ring, on a cord, up to the bull's head and over the horns.

Ken Boddy, Dick Bland and George Allen, among others, worked at Putteridge Bury Estate at one time, still as full of fun as when they were at school. A favourite trick of theirs was to entice some unsuspecting person to visit a wood there in the evening, under the pretext that it was the best time to kill rooks. The victim would enter the wood with a borrowed shotgun, get well under the nests scattered everywhere, and fire up into them. The result was a huge flock of rooks suddenly taking to flight, and in their panic dispensing excreta as they left the nests. This fell like rain . . . and the victim came out of the wood covered all over with large white spots, and swearing like a Trooper!

In 1919, the Rev. Canon Francis Aidan Hibbert was appointed Rector and took a great interest in the youth of the village. For quite a long time, Ken, Dick and Ted Holmes acted as servers at church. It is difficult for one to imagine how these three ever kept out of mischief for the duration of a service. On special occasions they were joined by the Rector's sons, making six servers in all. Dressed in red cassocks and lace-edged surplices, they took part in a type of service quite alien to many village people, causing quite a stir for some time.

Soon after his arrival, Mr Hibbert arranged a procession to Putteridge Bury to celebrate the end of the Great War. At the head of this rode Captain Holland Hibbert on a white horse accompanied by a man playing a cornet. Village children were dressed in replicas of the national costumes of the Allied nations. At Putteridge, there were sports, teas, dancing and, naturally, a beer tent which was well patronised as one can imagine by pipe-smoking, be-whiskered men dressed in their Sunday best, letting down their hair for a few hours.

Upon leaving that night a red glow over towards Luton was noticed, causing Bert Aylott to remark: "Looks like the buggers are having a good time there!" It was later learned that the Town Hall at Luton had been burned down and riot squads of police and soldiers called in. Reports that many innocent people going about their business that evening had received a whop on the head from a truncheon were rife in the village.

The Wesleyan Chapel had strong support during these days,

Fred Godfrey's daughter Ella playing a harmonium. There was also quite a strong Sunday School. At such special services as harvest festival, Ted Holmes and Co. were inclined to play truant from the C. of E. evensong and attend chapel, always aiming to get there early enough to get the front seats in a small gallery which extended from the entrance end. Micky Goodge, "Snipe" Dellar and others made a point of having some nuts or something similar in their pockets. On these occasions, the chapel music was provided by a band from Luton with plenty of brass. The idea of the nuts was to try to score a shot down the large, inviting mouth of the euphonium, or some such instrument, pomp-pomping away down below . . . which was rather disconcerting to the player, after a few nuts had found their way into the mouthpiece and created a rattle! Then David Coles would go up to the gallery with a little stick and sort the culprits out. After the festival, there would be a sale of the produce which, one might have guessed, the lads attended, though for what purpose has never been divulged.

After they had left school and were working, they had money of their own, perhaps for the first time in their lives, and like teenagers of any generation they met together; on Sundays at the Silver Lion to partake of ginger wine, pop and cigarettes. Up to the closing time of 2 pm they would each contribute one penny and purchase packets of cigarettes which had "fag cards" in them, each one being numbered. According to the size of the gang, each would have a series of numbers.

Then a draw would be made and the holder of the number on the card drawn from the packet would have the cigarettes. Sometimes a run of luck would enable one lad to come out with a pocket full of them, which he would then trade at a cheap rate to anyone who required them or barter in exchange for chocolate and sweets.

After this, a walk along the Hitchin road to the "Flints" — a small group of cottages — as far as "Darky" Dyer's little shop and one-pump garage there, where more pop would be consumed. If there was no sign of any Offley gang (there was quite a bit of needle between the villages, though not quite the amount that existed earlier) the lads would then walk by the windmill footpath to the Hoo, there to sit down and speak of the things that boys have always spoken of or play "pitch and toss" under a beech tree until tea-time.

With the end of the war and the subsequent return of those who had served, there was formed an organisation called the Discharged

Soldiers and Sailors Federation, or as it was popularly labelled "D.S. and S." The village branch set out to raise money to purchase a disused Army hut from Biscot Camp as a community centre. This was eventually erected on the new recreation ground which had been given by Mr Clutterbuck, of Putteridge Bury, as a safe place for children to play, free from the danger of a growing traffic problem and as a sports ground for villagers. The hut was grandly named the Victory Hall, and for many, many years did its job well enough.

The D.S. and S. also provided indoor games and a billiard table in the old Reading Room for the use of a men's club. The Reading Room served as headquarters for many activities, Bible classes, library, clothing club and a school to name but a few. It also housed a club before the 14-18 war, although not much is known of this, except that Oswald Bodsworth or "Oswald Bod" as he was known — who later emigrated to Australia — was concerned with its organisation, as was also Jimmy Little, father of "Biggy" Little.

The club organised by the D.S. and S. was active for quite a long time, and opened during the winter evenings from Monday to Friday. For a small annual subscription and about sixpence a week members could partake of billards, bagatelle, draughts, darts, cards, reading and dominoes. Horace Davis would sometimes take his gramophone and George Allen and Ted their banjoes for a tuneful, if not melodious, evening.

Needless to say, many were the tricks played. A favourite one was to sneak out, climb on to a well adjoining the end wall of the Reading Room, and place a sack over the chimney pot, thus causing much cursing down below as members fought for breath in the resulting clouds of black smoke; or around November Fifth dropping a cannon firework down the blessed chimney "to sort the buggers out".

About this time, Ted owned an old, cylinder gramophone, the records for which were made from beeswax, and the lads discovered that they could be cleaned off with paraffin and by fixing a bent pin on to the reproducing disc, they could record by singing or shouting down the "horn". One can imagine, by now, what sort of things were reproduced. They were so bad, in fact, that Ted dare not play the thing at home!

While playing billiards, "Titner" Coles would walk by the scoreboard with a cue innocently slung over a shoulder and either push his opponent's score back or his own forward, so the committee placed the board over the table on the roof truss. Then "Titner" found that due to the floor being timber-suspended, he could trot from one side to the other and thereby affect the run of the balls, enticing his opponent's ball away from a pocket or his own into one. How this act was remedied, however, has never been disclosed. Perhaps only one other person found out!

When the game "put and take" became the rage it was played each evening at the club with cigarettes as the stakes. "Titner" had the bright idea that if he kept a stock just to play with, he could use them over and over again. This he did, always taking a new one, or more, whenever the top said take and putting one or more of his stock into the pool when told to put, but unfortunately for "Titner" others soon caught on, to such an extent that in the end they were playing for little more than half empty papers of dry tobacco!

Later, the club and its equipment moved into the Victory Hall.

The Reading Room was also for a time used as living accommodation. A George Roast and family moved to the village and eventually lived in what used to be the bakehouse. Until then, it was probably his family that lived in the Reading Room, but this was before the D.S. and S. took over because George Roast was a member of the men's club.

Some years ago, the Reading Room, the beginnings of which are unknown, was demolished, though for what reason has not yet become evident. It should be recorded that in 1922 Canon Hibbert published a book called "The Story of a Small Village", setting out, in a most attractive way, the early history of the village from the time of the Domesday Survey in 1086, right through to the re-building of St. Peter's Church in 1870/71. It is an interesting story of prosperity and poverty, of basking in Royal acknowledgement to almost becoming extinct because of the Black Death.

Chapter 8

Employment

A farm workers' day was from sunrise or 6 a.m. to 5.30 or 6 p.m., and at haytime and harvest, until sunset; in 1904, Etty Payne worked from 7 a.m. until 8 p.m. at Lilley Laundry; Susan Bland often stayed at Putteridge Mansion until one or two in the morning, and for others in domestic service hours were just as long. The type of employment to be had in the village varied from domestic service and gardening to farm and estate work, with the odd gamekeeper thrown in for good measure.

The first part of the saying "Early to bed, early to rise makes a man healthy, wealthy and wise" was certainly true for the farm worker of the late nineteenth century, for very often he would have to rise at 4 a.m. to get to the farm in time to feed and water the horses and get teamed up ready for a 6 a.m. start in the fields, a break or "beaver" being taken around 10 o'clock. Time for finishing is not quite certain, but in some parts of Hertfordshire 2 p.m. would be the time the teams got back to the farm, having been expected to have ploughed, cut or cultivated one acre of land — deemed a day's work.

The horses would then be fed, watered and "racked up", that is made comfortable for the night, and the day's work was finished. But at haytime and harvest the men worked much later, as indeed they still do. An ordinary working day, at these times, was from 6 a.m. to 5 p.m. or thereabouts and at the busy times until 9 p.m. or later. Wages ranged from 11s. to 12s. 6d. a week, with perhaps another 10s. a week in the summer. A working week was normally from Monday to Saturday night, and the only holidays were Christmas Day and perhaps Good Friday. A hard life perhaps, according to our standards today, but are we, with ample leisure time, any happier?

The harvest about the turn of the century was usually contained in a month and was called "go in the month", when village boys were sometimes employed in the fields for this time.

Mechanical binders had just come out, but as far as I can ascertain were not in evidence in Lilley.

The first tractor plough was owned by Bert Facer, of Ward's Farm, and was followed by the local boys with much awe. This was about 1916.

As late as 1923, however, horses were still used for most farm duties, at least on one village farm, for Harry Coles was first employed on general farm duties in this year, at Manor Farm, and could remember the nine horses used there.

Harry started his working life at Trussells, the village bakers, and later went as horsemen to Col. T.G. Sowerby until 1923, when he took up general farm work for the Farr family — Robert Farr, and Tom and Fred, his sons, at Manor Farm.

His hours then were from 6 a.m. to 6.30 p.m., with a half-hour "beaver", one hour for dinner, and a 1 p.m. finish on Saturdays for 32s. per week. At haytime and harvest he received 2s. 6d. per hour overtime, which was worked until dusk. Three men on the farm were responsible for the horses — Harry, Arthur Weedon, who lived at Pump Cottages, and Will Mullion, who lived at Saunders Yard. Two other men were also employed, Cyril French and Fred Webb, as well as casual labour at the busy times.

A typical farming year in 1923 was: Harvest, cut by horse-drawn binders. Sheaves set in stooks. Carted and stacked, a stack of oats being threshed as soon as possible to be fed to the horses.

After harvest, some ploughing was done. Harry told me that two horses were used to draw a single-furrow plough, a ten-acre field being completed by three teams in just over three days.

After this spot of ploughing, mangolds for feeding the cattle were pulled. Four rows at a time were thrown into heaps, which were either covered over with leaves and left awhile, or carted immediately and clamped. The mangold-pulling was normally followed by the rest of the threshing — undertaken, naturally, by A.T. Oliver's, of Wandon End.

February and March were the months when the clearing-out of all manure from crew yards took place. This valuable material was then clamped or spread on the mangold ground ready for the next season. Completed then was the rest of the ploughing for spring sowing, followed by hedging.

At haytime, clover was cut first, followed by the meadow grass; again with a horse-drawn grass machine. The hay was turned by hand, and put straight into stacks.

How those girls sang as they washed and scrubbed and rubbed the sheets and pillow cases, tablecloths and shirt fronts at Lilley Laundry about the turn of the century. So said Etty Payne, who worked there from 1904 to 1914.

The laundry was owned by Lizzie Taylor, and was located at the cottages in Balk Lane. Washing was accepted from all the big houses in the area, and was transported in huge hampers loaded on to carts.

Etty Payne lived-in and worked from 7 a.m. to 8 p.m. with a break for lunch. For these twelve or so hours a day she received the princely sum of 4s. a week. At the end of her ten years she was receiving 7s. 6d. a week. Etty's workmates were Margaret Salmon (Miss Taylor's niece), Esther Clarke and Sarah Brown, plus a few others who did the heavy washing, and later on Gertie Bodsworth, Annie Birkett and Beattie Clarke joined the happy throng.

The washing was done in large wooden tubs filled with rain water. If this was not available then the water was drawn from a well in the garden. Large, scrubbed tables were used for ironing.

Collars and shirt fronts, invariably stiffly starched, were ironed with a polishing iron, which had a rounded bottom for this purpose. Frills, of which there were many, were tackled with a gofering iron, more like the tongs once used by ladies for setting their hair.

Some of the prices for a first-class job, as recalled by Etty, were: Collars 1d., shirt fronts 2d., shirts 4d., sheets 2d., large tablecloths (three to four yards in length) 4d.

As well as farm, estate and domestic work, straw plaiting — as we have already seen — played a very important part as extra employment in the village, and the income derived therefrom by the womenfolk made a welcome addition to the family budget and made possible a few luxuries.

Protracted investigation has revealed that very much straw plait was actually made in Lilley, the finished article being sold mostly to Gray's, of Barbers Lane, Luton. Liz Allen, was an expert in the art, as was Rose Roffe who remembered plaiting and could recall using a plaiting mill — two stone rollers worked by a handle through which the straw was threaded to soften it. A plaiting mill is to be found still at Lilley House.

Eliza Webb was another of an earlier age who was an expert plaiter, her nimble fingers still weaving in her 93rd year. Eliza shared one of the almshouses with Betsy Watson, also a plaiter. Betsy plaited with coarse straws and Eliza with split straws, producing a finer plait. Both sold them to a Mr. Dawson, of Luton, who collected them in his pony and trap.

Edwin Grey has described straw plaiting as he remembered it being done at Harpenden. He also mentions a plaiting school at Harpenden. Several people have testified to the fact that such a school existed in Lilley.

Chapter 9

The Village School

According to these testimonies there were three schools in Lilley that taught children to plait. An old lady called Fanny Ebbs is reputed to have kept a small school at Church Cottage where, for 2d. a week, children were taught to read and write . . . and, of course, to plait. There was supposedly such a school at "No. 55" — which once housed the village post office and blacksmith — and yet again the local "grapevine" has it that a Miss Eaton ran a much earlier Dame School at Church Cottage.

It has not been possible to uncover any documentary records of plaiting schools in Lilley, so we must assume that, despite conflicting stories, plaiting was taught sometime, somewhere in the village.

The first real piece of educational documentation shows that a school of sorts was started in 1865 in the Reading Room, where children were taught by Mr. Jennings, the Curate. After he left, this work was carried on by Rector Haviland and Matthew Feakes for five winters, before a National Society School was built and opened in 1875, the first Head being Miss Esther Cundall, who was to occupy that position for thirty-three years, having been in the village for two years prior to the school's opening.

By 1890, education in the three R's was universal, or nearly so, but many countrymen regarded it as no more than a mixed blessing. There was so much he had to learn that was not contained in books.

Captain Vye, in Hardy's "The Return of the Native", must have expressed the opinion of many Lilley people when he declared: "There's too much of that there sending to school these days! It only does harm. Every gatepost and barn door you come to is sure to have some bad word or other chalked upon it by the young rascals; a woman can hardly pass for shame sometimes". Ted Holmes can tell a story of the time when he wrote something detrimental to the squire — which I will not repeat here — on Trussell's barn opposite the school. After being uncovered as the culprit, Ted had to spend several hours removing the results of his wit!

Lilley C. of E. School, unfortunately closed in 1984. Now a block of flats.   BO

A later picture of the school. Notice the fine Victorian chimneys are missing here.

Lilley School as it is now.

In 1890, if one walked through the village, one might have had difficulty in identifying boys and girls because custom and household economy often demanded that boys should wear their older sisters' clothes as they grew into them. This did not produce the taunting and bloody noses that one might suppose, as other little boys in the village suffered the same indignity, but without feeling it was any great affront to their manhood. The age when a boy graduated into trousers depended on whether, and when, the family possessed a pair that would fit him.

The former village school possessed some very interesting records that unfortunately did not start until 1908, in which year about a hundred children attended, under the firm hand of Miss E.A. Randall, who had succeeded Esther Cundall as head. In this same year, having reached twelve years of age, five children gained exemption certificates and were able to leave . . . to add their small income to the family budget. An exemption certificate proved that a child had learned just enough to be excused further tuition.

In 1908 the school closed for only one week in the summer for what was termed "a harvest holiday", when the majority of the boys helped gather in the grain harvest; earlier, as we have seen, some boys were given leave for a whole month for this purpose. A serious

A group of village schoolchildren before the turn of the century. The author's grandmother is third from the right, middle row.

outbreak of ringworm occurred, which did not, apparently, affect George Brown, for we read: "For displaying very violent temper, George Brown flogged across knickerbockers". He received the same treatment the next day as well; in fact, hardly a day passed without him being reprimanded in some way. Once he was locked in the boys' porch for misbehaving. Not to be outdone, George lifted up the doormat, and shook it, and shook it until the porch looked like the inside of a vacuum cleaner. Needless to say, he had to be released, though the temptation to let him suffocate must have passed through the mind of Miss Randall!

The year 1909 was remarkable in that the school was closed for several weeks because of an outbreak of measles; at one time fifty-one children being affected. The punishment book reveals that Sidney Coles received four strokes of the cane for being "most idle", and Harry Stillwell was flogged across the back for "great disobedience".

Three children received watches for five years' perfect attendance — Doris and Cyril French and Fred Brown. And it was "perfect" attendance at that, for the registers were taken twice a day, first thing in the morning and again after lunch. This incentive was inaugurated by Hertfordshire County Council in 1904. A medal was also given for one year's perfect attendance. It was made of bronze, and bore on one side the county crest, and on the other the name of the school and the recipient.

An old boy, David Trussell, was ordained priest in 1910 by the Bishop of Oxford, and later sailed in the Kenilworth Castle, to begin work in Johannesberg, South Africa.

There was an outbreak of whooping cough and croup in 1911. From the punishmnent book, we see that Harry Coles received four strokes of the cane for "Behaving badly when left at work for one minute".

Mrs. T.M. Clutterbuck, from Putteridge Bury, visited the school in 1912, and gave clogs to those children who needed re-shoeing.

The school closed once more in 1914 because of an outbreak of scarlet fever and was disinfected from top to bottom. "For persistently disturbing others in his class by making grimaces", Stanley Goodge received four strokes, and for "snobbery" Bertha Spicer received one stroke. At first, it would seem that this punishment was unduly harsh for a trait that today is well nigh universal. But was it harsh? My dictionary gives this definition of the word snob: "A vulgar person who apes gentility". Not a characteristic, surely, to be encouraged in a Church school?

During 1918 the boys of Lilley School appeared to be out of control, for we read that "the village policeman was called in to speak to some of the boys who were being very rude". One can only assume the long arm of the law had the desired effect! At this time, towards the end of the Great War, with many village men away at the front, much time was spent in the hayfields by the bigger boys, and horse chestnuts were gathered for munitions. From the punishment book we learn that Charles Read received three strokes on the hand and a thrashing as well for "sending a cheeky message to me when I sent Dick Titmuss to fetch him", and William Weedon received a caning for "sticking a pen in another boy's ear".

Teaching must have been very hard work in days gone by (not implying that it's easy now, of course), but then there was very little apparatus for the children to use, and they were expected to sit still in rows on long forms. There was no room for any activity.

About 1910, every day at the village school began with a scripture lesson lasting about 45 minutes. Children were certainly well grounded in this subject. Maud Holmes remembers some pictures which were used to illustrate these lessons. Very wonderful she thought they were, too, being highly coloured and large.

Once a year, the "Scripture Inspector" visited the school to examine the children. This was a most important event, and both school and scholars had to look their best. When Maud was a small child the "Inspector" was the Rev. Basil Reay, tall, rather grim-looking and dressed in black. When he entered, accompanied by the Rector, the scholars rose with one accord and chorused "Good morning, sir". The children in the "big room" were furnished with pens and paper and told to write out The Lord's Prayer, My Duty Towards God and My Duty Towards My Neighbour, according to their age. Meanwhile "Sir" went to the infant room to talk to the youngsters, then they were allowed to go home. The other classes were questioned on the syllabus set for the year, and any child who did well was given a certificate signed by Mr. Reay. If a child did well for three years it was given a much more elaborate certificate signed by both Mr. Reay and the Rector.

Maud cannot remember being taught to read, but by six or seven she could read fluently. It is probable that the teaching methods used then would be condemned today; indeed, it is certain, but nevertheless most children could read, write legibly, spell and do a certain amount of arithmetic. What was missing, one feels, was equal opportunity, though this was not necessarily the fault of educationalists, but rather the fault of a social system that made it impossible for children to continue their education, many, because of poverty, having to leave school at twelve years of age.

There was a small harmonium in the infant room which Charlotte Titmuss laboriously pedalled with her feet and played with one hand. What the children's efforts must have sounded like is, perhaps, beyond imagination!

The village school was built, as was the church, partly by the generosity of the Rev. Arthur Coles Haviland and by others (including the National Society), in 1875. Esther Cundall was appointed as the first Headmistress, but she had retired before Maud went to school. Her place (as we have seen) was taken by Miss Randall, who was terribly crippled by arthritis. She was not really well enough to keep good discipline, and some of the bigger boys took advantage of her infirmity.

To many children it must have seemed that Mr. Haviland's favourite colour was dark red. The lower part of the inner walls of the church and school were painted in this colour. The windows of the school were placed high up in the wall so that no child could look out. The two rooms were "heated" by a coal fire in each room. If one were lucky enough to sit somewhere near the fire it was not too bad, but at the back of the room, one froze. At one time, in fact, all the children were sent home because of a shortage of coal.

On one of the infant room walls was a diagram of the underground home of a mole, and pictures of a dairy, with thick cream on top of shallow pans. If the scholars were very good they were allowed to play with a doll's house, which they thought was marvellous. It lived on top of a cupboard.

It is sometimes said that as one gets older, one forgets wet and cold weather and remembers only long, fine sunny days. Maud Holmes remembers plenty of those, but also she remembers some dreadful thunderstorms, when the lamps were lit, the blinds pulled down, any article made of steel being covered up or put away, and Charlotte Titmuss taking off her steel-rimmed spectacles, and thinking how strange she looked without them.

Girls and boys entered the school in those days through the front of the two porches, which, at the time of writing, still exist, the boys through the left one and the girls through the right. In the middle of the long back wall of the "big room" hung a large portrait of Rector Haviland and another of Esther Cundall standing on a school step. On the left wall hung two cases, one containing specimens of the cotton plant and the other of cocoa beans. Geometrical shapes adorned the top of a cupboard. In this room there was a piano. Long desks and forms fixed to the floor were arranged in three groups; green curtains could be pulled in between. All the children sat facing the road, and the teachers stood in front of them. There was very little individual attention. Some children started school before they were five years old and most left at fourteen, some earlier.

The toilets and washing facilities were very primitive. The back yard of the school grounds was divided by a high wall, with girls' lavatories on the right and boys' on the left, and woe betide any boy who trespassed on forbidden ground! A pump provided water for washing. The playground at this time was just a rather rough, stony surface, with a high hedge bordering the road with a large witch-hazel tree growing in one corner. This gave welcome shade on hot, sunny days. Blue periwinkle grew in a border and a flag pole was erected in another corner. On Empire Day and St. Peter's Day the scholars marched around the playground and saluted the flag; patriotism then was something to be cherished, not ridiculed, as is sometimes the case today.

Many games were played in the school grounds and on the road; games that have practically died out now. There were the seasonal ones such as bowling hoops, skipping, spinning tops, etc., and others which were played at any time: Marbles, tip-tap-toe, jinks, tag, gilly liftings, gilly holdings, moonlight-starlight, fox and hounds, in and out the windows, and many others.

A bell used to hang on the wall outside the boys' porch. It was rung five minutes before school began as a warning to latecomers and then again when school was to begin.

In the depths of winter, when Doozley Pond was frozen over and there were splendid slides right across it, children went on sliding until the last possible moment and then went running and panting up the hill from the pond and into the playground, just in the nick of time!

Miss Randall eventually retired through ill-health, and Miss Beatrice Olive Rendell was appointed Headmistress in 1914. She was then about twenty-four, although to the children she seemed quite old!

If ever a woman created a revolution in a school she did. She had been trained at Whitelands College, in London, and was full of the new methods. She was rather short and plump, with long dark hair which was always falling down over her lovely violet eyes.

From the word go, things began to move. No more pandering to naughty big boys — the cane worked overtime! Maud Holmes was in the "second class" when Miss Rendell first came to the village, and she absolutely dreaded going up into her class. But when she did, what a revelation! Miss Rendell was an excellent teacher and simply lived for her work. Whatever she attempted to do or teach she did as an expert. Needlework, knitting, book-binding and leather-work she taught, as well as the basic subjects in a school curriculum. She had a very good contralto voice and was keen on music, singing, dancing and drama. Of course, she was not perfect. She was always late. School never started or finished on time and teachers who worked under her had rather a sticky time.

At the beginning of the First World War, food and clothing became scarce. On many autumn mornings the bigger children trooped out to scour the hedgerows for blackberries with which to make jam for the soldiers, and were paid a small sum per pound. A boy named Clifford Farrow, however, lived in a keeper's cottage by the wood and he used to take to school big baskets of fruit picked in the wood. How his friends envied him!

Many evenings were spent by the girls and Miss Rendell cutting out and stitching garments made from cast-off clothing. Walking home afterwards in the dark, the girls would see the searchlights probing the sky, great long fingers of light, bent on hastening destruction.

The fact that a war was being fought, did not stop the children giving concerts. In Miss Randall's time they had given small entertainments at Temperance meetings, where the Rector was chairman, and various children recited and sang, but now they were much more ambitious, performing sketches and plays and dressing up. Eventually they graduated to Shakespeare, performing "A

Midsummer Night's Dream" in the village school upon a stage built by Harry Taylor, under the direction of Beatrice Rendell, and to an audience of villagers who had never seen the like before!

In those days, most children left school at fourteen years of age, but there was a scheme under which children of twelve or so could sit for an examination at Hitchin. If they passed it they were allowed to leave and start work.

On March 28, 1916, several children from the school were driven to Hitchin in horse dealer Jabez Cain's wagonette to take the examination. It was Hitchin market day. During the afternoon it began to snow, and by the time the children had finished, the wind had risen to gale force and was blowing the snow in blinding flurries. Jabez started for home with his load of scholars, but the blizzard was so bad that Jabez and the children had to walk home through the storm. Luckily the wind was behind them. The village lost scores of its trees that day and as a result a saw mill was started by the Squire at Butterfield Green to cope with the fallen wood.

In the 1920's, timetables were drawn up by the Headmistress for each class. Every day had its special lessons, usually lasting about half an hour. School began at nine o'clock with prayers and a hymn, followed by "calling the register". Then came the Scripture lesson until 9.45. Arithmetic always followed Scripture, and then playtime, after which there would be history, geography or reading lessons according to the timetable. The children went home at twelve noon for lunch and returned at two o'clock. The afternoon lessons were usually drawing, sewing, handwork, modelling, nature study, singing and dancing. Some of the older children learned leather-work and rug-making.

Miss Rendell was very keen on teaching needlework, and many a girl she taught must have blessed her in later life. She would gather the class around a big, flat-topped table (which now stands in the church vestry) and demonstrate how to cut out a garment, how to place the pattern and how to save material. Patterns were often made by the girls themselves and drawn to scale in a needlework book. All sorts of processes were learned: How to put a gusset in a skirt, how to make a buttonhole, how to tack, hem, backstitch and run; how to make seams, run, fill and darn, and so on. Long black stockings, full of holes, were borrowed for the pupils to practice on, and it seemed that each time a girl thought she had filled up every hole, the mistress poked a finger through another!

Ted Holmes' earliest recollections of school are as an infant much impressed by a large picture on one wall of the infants' room, displaying all sorts of animals with a large elephant in the middle; the clock with moveable hands on another wall — used to teach children the time — and a large dolls' house. Later on, he remembers Miss Randall talking at length about a new ship which was so designed that it could not sink, and the great distress after the Titanic had struck an iceberg and sunk on its maiden voyage; and her subsequent quotation from the Bible, given as advice:

"Let he who thinketh he standeth take heed, lest he fall."

Upon the death of King Edward VII every child at school was given a black armband to wear.

At the Coronation of King George V, on May 6, 1910, there were great festivities on the village Green and in Trussells' Meadow, where stood the former Post Office, with a large marquee, a band, dancing and sports, which included a greasy pole, upon the top of which was placed a veal ham, the idea being that the competitor who could shin to the top of the pole won the ham. Sid Clark managed to do this, amid great applause. His name is now recorded on the War Memorial. John Trussell was another village lad who did well. He was very good as a sprinter. He, too, was killed in the Great War.

The festivities on the Green included a cross-country three and a half mile race, won by Arthur Webb, son of "Piney" Webb, who lived at "Topend". He won easily over a course from the Sowerby Arms, via Ward's Wood Lane and the Icknield Way and back to Trussells' Meadow for the tape, but collapsed after finishing.

Another old event Ted remembers was a fair in Cherry Meadow by Balk Lane, then used by Laban Lines as grazing for his cows. This was probably the last of the old Statty fairs which were followed later by fairs in the Midland Meadow. It was at one such event that Ted first had a drink of beer. Pressed to it by Lizzy Martin, he felt quite a man — although he did not like the taste very much!

About this time, the village boasted a very good church choir, with a full row of boys and a full row of men each side. The choirmaster best remembered was Mr. Cain, known to the boys as "Cainy", who held choir practice in the school each week. The Rector then was the Rev. Edward Genge, who also attended, and if the boys were absent or late, a house visit resulted. A quick search into the most likely hiding places was made for those not found at home.

Perhaps at this stage it would be a good idea to mention nick-names. Most men and boys had one, some being known by a shortened version of their Christian or surname. About the village could be found Dick "Chauffeur" Bland, so called because of his desire to become a car driver; Ken "Roger" Boddy, named after a

Roger Claridge from Mangrove, a very good footballer, whose style Ken endeavoured to copy. There was also Stan "Micky" Goodge, Eddie "Scrubby" Dellar, Fred "Snipe" Dellar, his father "Punch" Dellar and Eddie Dellar's brother Archie "Pompey" Dellar.

Fred "Potick" Brown, so named because, when once reciting a poem, instead of saying "I put it in my pocket" he said "Potick" and the name stuck. George Allen earned the name "Cooby" because, while living in the house which used to be attached to Church Cottage, he fed the poultry at Church Farm to get pocket money. Others were Tom "Biggy" Little, Fred "Froggy" Day, Sid "Titner" Coles, brother of Harry "Hadge" Coles, Hubert "Mousy" Chapman, because he used to take mice to school in a matchbox and release them in class, Stan "Soger" Clark (a corruption of soldier), Cyril "General" French, Will "Reuben" Oliver, Arthur "Tut" Tuttleby, "Little Dick Sparrow" Titmuss.

Amongst the men were "Dusty" Trussell; the father of Sid Clark, who climbed the greasy pole, was called "Bobby Winkle" for some obscure reason. His elder son, a regular soldier, was called "Budgie". He married and brought home his bride, plus a crabby old parrot which would only screech. "Piney" Webb lived in the last house of a row of old Almshouses on the Hitchin Road. He was father of the Arthur Webb who won the cross-country race at the Coronation celebrations. Others were "Smasher" Payne, "Puffer" Bland, "Jammy" Coles, slate club, cricket and football secretary. The roadman was known as "Peggy" because he had a wooden leg. There were many others too numerous to mention, but the list must include four girls, not of this parish, who were known, rather unkindly perhaps, as "Sarah Instep", "Maulden Floe", "Annie Scrape" and "Emma Whoa Back".

For the lantern lectures and concerts which used to be given at school, chairs had to be brought up from the "New Room" at the Rectory to provide seating. A number of boys were given the job of fetching them, and each would carry six chairs at once, all the way. Those who could not were thought to be cissies. It was done this way: Two chairs were placed seat to seat on top of the head, with the legs of one back and front of the shoulders; then, from the four legs standing upright, four others were hung by their backs. So laden, the lads then staggered one behind the other down the Rectory drive and up the hill to the school.

One penny a week could be had from Fred Godfrey, the village postmaster, for transporting the "Luton News" from the butcher's to his shop each week by truck. They arrived with the "Skin Man's" vehicle. Newspapers then had to be collected from the post office, although these did not include any daily papers which were

Another village school group in the 1930s. Can yuo recognise any of them? The man on the right is Mr Milsom, the headmaster.   JT

Some more Lilley schoolchildren. This time on a nature walk with headmaster Derek Collins.   PC

Schoolchildren outside the school about 1943. MT

Country dancing in the playground of Lilley School in happier times. In fact, the date is May 11th, 1957. PC

unobtainable in the village, the "Luton News", "Lloyds Weekly News", "The Family Journal" and a comic called "Chips" being all that could be had, and they usually arrived days late, and were swapped around and swapped again, until they appeared very dog-eared indeed!

At one time, many village lads kept rabbits and went out in the fields and lanes gathering hogweed, dandelions and sowthistles for food, and grass to dry and use as litter. On one occasion, about tea-time, "Chauffeur" Bland, "Scrubby" Dellar and Ted Holmes were cutting grass with a sickle and collecting hogweed in Balk Lane.

During school that day the reading lesson had been a story dealing with strange and wild animals, and imaginations had run riot. Some children told of seeing a large, dog-like animal roaming around the churchyard; others had witnessed the loping strides of a six-legged giraffe with antlers; yet others had run for their lives from a snake with three heads and wings. All these stories had been forgotten, however, as the three boys busied themselves cutting grass and searching for food along this ancient track.

The evening was rather warm, so they took off their coats, but after what seemed only a short time realised it was getting dark, so collected their grass and hogweed and went to put on their coats and make for home.

It was then that "Scrubby" announced he was unable to find his coat. In the dim light, with the bats flittering here and there, they searched up and down the Balk with no success, and all the while growing more and more nervous as the tales told at school that day came flooding back into their minds.

Suddenly "Chauffeur" pointed out a dark, animal-like shape which appeared to be looking at them through the hedge some twenty yards lower down. The moon had risen by this time and a long pointed nose and shining eyes, which seemed to be watching the boys, grew more clear.

The "Thing" was between them and home, and as they watched, it appeared to move. After some debate "Scrubby" suggested throwing a piece of wood at it and making a bolt for home and searching for his coat in the morning. It was agreed that Ted was perhaps the best thrower, and should creep a little closer and try to hit the "Thing". He reluctantly agreed to do this and scored a good hit. The "Thing" crumpled up, just like a coat — "Scrubby's" coat, in fact!

Chapter 10

Some More Background

As a toddler, a child's main diet was often composed of bread and milk and home-made soup.

Church attendance was strictly imposed, three times a day being the custom in most households. Sunday School in the afternoon was taken by the day-school teachers . . . and woe betide any child that misbehaved.

Discipline in and out of the home was often very strict. Child psychology then was simple, merely consisting of a good hefty clout! At school, records show that a lad would be "thrashed across the knickerbockers" for next to nothing.

Lessons at school were nearly always learnt parrot-fashion by the whole class repeating the lessons out loud. In summertime, forms and chairs were taken into an adjoining meadow and set under a big "Nut Hazel" tree for children to enjoy the air and sun. Discipline, too, by all accounts, was more relaxed out here. Perhaps there was more room to escape the cane!

If any of the teachers were met in the village after school, during the weekends or during holidays they were all respectfully addressed as "Miss" — as indeed most of them literally were.

Jobs were allotted in house and garden for which a child might receive a ha'porth of sweets, such as "Oh Mother Look" obtained from Luton's open-air market. Another favourite was a farthing-worth of "Vinegar Flats" or piping hot faggots from Lizzie Cain's shop that is now Ulpha House.

Various other jobs were undertaken that brought in the odd copper or two. Delivering meat for Young's the butchers was a Saturday morning job. A pony and trap was used as transportation to King's Walden, Tea Green and Mangrove. Then there was milk to be churned at Church Farm for "Shaddy" Atkins, and one or two paper rounds on a Sunday morning.

Besides the usual games, children in the village had various events which drew their interest. The annual Hertfordshire Hunt

Church Farm house. Very much the same today. What is missing now is the pond shown in the foreground. *BO*

"meet" at a village inn was an excuse for boys to play truant from school; to tear wildly over field and meadow, through wood and spinney — to be followed by a sound "whacking" at school next day.

Another exciting venture was a trip to Galley Hill or Telegraph Hill to see the early aeroplanes pass over while taking part in air races. Considering the height of both these hills and the height at which those old box-like biplanes flew, one can imagine that a rare old din occurred when those "magnificent men in their flying machines" passed overhead.

One or two events still stick in the minds of older residents. One day a chimney beam in a cottage on the Green caught fire. Because of the difficulty of obtaining the services of a fire brigade, neighbours climbed upon the roof and threw buckets of water down the chimney. The fire was successfully extinguished but the ensuing mess in the room apparently defies description. This cottage, incidentally, was the Sunday morning rendezvous for some real old village characters, who were in the habit of frequenting the cellar, there to partake of some strong ale, a pipeful of tobacco, and a real old chinwag, seated on overturned half-barrels, amongst the rats, spiders and cobwebs — out of earshot, too, one suspects, of their hardworking spouses!

A fire at Mortgrove Farm is still remembered, not so much for the fire itself, but for the horse-drawn tender (perhaps the one from Offley) that flew hell-for-leather through the village. Several fires in the wood behind the church, either during or just after the war, are still spoken of, because some right raging infernos they proved to be. After they had died out, village people were allowed to collect as much wood as they liked, a facility that was taken up with much alacrity. Villagers have always had a yen for wooding, something, I think, that must be in their make-up.

The horse-drawn mail vans from Luton caused some interest as well because they also were driven at a furious pace. The story is told that one day a post office horse dropped dead from sheer exhaustion. The poor beast, so it is said, had been worked to death. It is very doubtful, however, if this is possible. These beautiful animals, that must surely rank as man's real best friend, are extremely tough, and if properly looked after would never die from hard work.

Most villages have one or two ghost stories to tell. The one here concerns the ruins of the old Parsonage House, that is supposed to be the home of a good old rural spook, that walks the old Rectory grounds after the witching hour is passed. Children always shunned passing this ruin. If they did it was always at full gallop. As far as I know, no one has ever seen a ghost, headless, draped in chains or otherwise. But who knows, one might exist!

A delightful superstition in Hertfordshire around 1868 was the rite of the "Bible and Key". Two village maidens, desirous of ascertaining who were to be their lovers, would get a Bible and a house door key, the latter at that time being much larger than those now in use. The locking end of the key was placed on verses six and seven of chapter eight of the Song of Solomon:

Set me as a seal upon your heart,
as a seal upon your arm;
for love is strong as death,
jealousy is cruel as the grave.
Its flashes are flashes of fire,
a most vehement flame.
Many waters cannot quench love,
Neither can floods drown it.
If a man offered for love
all the wealth of his house,
it would be utterly scorned.

The Bible was then closed, and tied tightly round so that the key was kept in close contact with the verses. The girls now sat closely opposite each other and each extended a forefinger through the ring of the key so that both Bible and key were freely suspended. Starting with the letter A, one girl would say:

> If A be the first letter of my love's name
> May the bible turn round
> And the key do the same.

If nothing resulted, the second girl would repeat the formula, and so they would continue with the letters of the alphabet. If the Bible and key turned at, say, C or G it was assumed that the lover's name was Charles or George, or a name beginning with those letters.

The late Mr Edwin Grey, author of "Cottage Life in a Hertfordshire Village", responsible for the above little story, actually saw the turning of the Bible and key, but the agency causing it was not apparent.

St. Valentine's Day:

"In many parts of Hertfordshire", says a writer in Hone's Year Book, "it is customary for the poor and middle classes of children to assemble together on St. Valentine's Day in some part of the town or village where they live, and to proceed from thence to the house of the chief personage of the place, who throws them wreaths and true lovers' knots from the window, with which they adorn themselves. Two or three of the girls then select one of the youngest among them, generally a boy, whom they deck out more gaily than the rest and, placing him at the head, march forward in the greatest state imaginable, at the same time playfully singing:

> Good morrow to you Valentine,
> Curl your locks as I do mine,
> Two before and three behind,
> Good morrow to you Valentine.

"This they repeat under the windows of all the houses they pass, and the inhabitants are seldom known to refuse a mite to reward the merry soliciting of these juvenile serenaders. They begin their pranks as early as six o'clock in the morning."

There is an old belief, still cherished by many country folk, that whatever you are doing when you first hear the cuckoo you will do most frequently during the rest of the year. And if an unmarried man hears the cuckoo, the legend runs that "he will remain a bachelor as many years as calls of the cuckoo he hears". Some people will turn their money over for luck when they hear the cuckoo. This is supposed to double a man's fortune before the end of the year. In medieval times they believed the cuckoo to be a god that had assumed mortal shape. To kill one was a crime of the first magnitude.

April 14 is still known in many country districts as Cuckoo Day, and Heathfield Fair in Sussex, held on that day, is known as Cuckoo Fair. Some two centuries ago East Anglian labourers used to celebrate the cuckoo's coming by leaving their work as soon as its note was heard echoing through the springtime woods, and spend the rest of the day drinking "cuckoo ale". Another cuckoo superstition says that a girl may find out whether she is going to marry a dark man or a fair one by going out in the early morning and listening. As soon as the cuckoo calls she must take off her left shoe and there she will find a hair from the head of her future bridegroom!

In some parts of Britain you may still hear quoted these old lines about the cuckoo:

In April he shows his bill.
In May he sings night and day.
In June he altereth his tune.
In July he prepares to fly.
In August go he must.
In September he's gone, remember
In October if you hear him, you're not sober.

Two which were very popular in Hertfordshire during the last century were set to music, and the second was still sung by schoolchildren a few years ago, and maybe still is:

The cuckoo he sings in April.
The cuckoo he sings in May.
The cuckoo he sings in June.
In July he flies away.

And

He comes in mid-April.
He sings in mid-May.
With the first cock of May
Flies the cuckoo away.

Perhaps the most ancient and picturesque of the harvest field customs, and one which has been missed more than any other, is that of gleaning. The unforgettable story of Ruth gleaning "amid the alien corn" has inspired both poet and painter. It is indeed a sad loss that the groups of women and children gleaning the golden grain in the village fields are no longer seen. The September sunshine, mellow and still very warm; the hedgerows and trees, tinged with the first colours of Autumn; the blackberries, red hips and haws; crab apples in abundance; the elderberry, providing food for all kinds of birds. The sound of happy laughter mingling with the peace of those stubbled fields, still producing the grain of sustenance, as if reluctant to yield once more to the frosts of winter. That is a romantic view, of course. Very often, no doubt, it was raining!

After a cornfield had been carted it was thrown open and anyone so inclined could go and pick up any corn that had been left. It was well worth gleaning so long as the reaping had been done with a scythe; when the binder was introduced the "harvest" was not so plentiful, but still very much worth the effort.

Almost all the land of the parish (as it is now, in fact) was ploughed and cultivated for cereal crops, and much of the flour consumed in the house was ground from corn gleaned on the surrounding fields. It was customary then for most housewives to make their own bread.

Bread made by the Trussell family in the village bakehouse was delicious. Over at Breachwood Green potato water was used for making it. Small potatoes being washed and boiled in their skins and then sieved. Lumps of newly baked bread were often eaten with cheese at break times on the farm or in the fields.

Corresponding to the home-made loaf, the home-cured flitch of bacon then constituted a mainstay of village fare, to the extent that it was customary to speak of beef, mutton, etc., purchased from the butcher as "fresh meat". No thrifty villager could entertain life without one or more pigs in the sty. The remains of such a sty can still be seen in Jack Farnham's garden.

On a Friday afternoon, some time between 1904 and 1908, a unique tea and entertainment was witnessed at the village school; unique because nothing like it had ever been held before. A local Press report stated:

"A novel tea and entertainment were given in the National School on Friday afternoon and evening by the school children. It was called the 'Acorn Tea' and originated in the following manner. During the acorn season the governess, Miss E. Cundall, induced the children to pick up acorns in their spare time, and bring them to her. Having gathered all they could, the whole of them were sold and the proceeds spent in providing a tea for their parents. One hundred were invited, school children attending from fifty homes. There was an excellent repast to which the guests did ample justice. The tea over, an evening's entertainment had been prepared and arranged by the governess; Miss Randall (assistant governess) and the scholars. A long programme, full of interesting items, had been drawn up by the children, the whole capitally rendered and well received. Right well did the little folk take up their various parts, the bright eyes and happy faces testifying how much they enjoyed the role of artistes.

"Never was there a more sympathetic or appreciative audience, composed as it was of the parents of the young performers. Several ladies and gentlemen added to the evening's enjoyment by kindly singing songs at intervals, thus giving the little ones time to rest between their parts. The following droll pieces were the most mirth provoking and caused more than one jolly laugh: 'My Pottet', 'Topsy-Turvy Song', 'The Quack', 'The Forgetful Man', 'Our Baby', 'An Obliging Customer' and a sneezing song.

"Two hours were pleasantly spent by all concerned, The Rector, the Rev. E.H. Genge, who presided, warmly thanked all who had taken part, congratulating Miss Cundall and Miss Randall upon the excellent result of their labour of love in their teaching and training the children out of school hours to be so useful to others. The audience endorsed these remarks by enthusiastic applause."

Chapter 11

Pheasant Shooting And All That

About the time the acorn tea and entertainment was being enjoyed in the school, local gentry and gamekeepers were preparing for a season's game shooting, and whether one agrees with it or not, always an integral part of village life. On most Saturdays in the season it has been possible over many years to hear the guns as the game is driven past and over them by beaters. In the old days the shooting party mostly comprised weekend guests, as the game books, dating back to 1884, show. In this year the estate supplied 1,554 partridge, 1,194 pheasant, 422 hares, 12,527 rabbits, four woodcock and 439 wood pigeons, totalling 16,140 items of game.

In 1895 we see the names of the shooting parties as: September 2, H.P. Greenwood, F.W. Fellowes, T.G., H.J. and F.H.A. Sowerby, Warden Hills, 118 partridge, twenty hares; September 27, J.G. Dewar, G. Oakley, C.B. Tylecote, T.F. Harrison, and the three Sowerbys, Lilley Bottom, 205 partridge, five hares, fifteen rabbits; November 15, F. Crawley, H.P. Greenwood, Col. Blackburn, F. Gosling and the three Sowerbys, Stubbocks and Bricket, one partridge, 313 pheasant, thirty-eight hares, 223 rabbits, four wood pigeons. 1896, January 15, Capt. T.G. Dewar, Col. Daniel, T. Harrison, and the three Sowerbys, The Park, 107 pheasant, 439 rabbits, seven wood pigeons. Nothing else is recorded then until 1907 when, on January 11, Col. Dewar, Harry Duff Gordon, Bill Fellowes and T.G. and H.J. Sowerby shot seventeen partridge, sixty-two pheasant, sixteen hares, five rabbits. 1908, April 1, ferret party obtained 690 rabbits. Shooting carried on during the Great War, although the names of the guns are not given.

Sir Felix Cassel's name appears for the first time on November 13, 1922, when the bag was fourteen partridge, 246 pheasant, twenty-seven hares, ten rabbits, four woodcock. Sir Felix was very keen on shooting and many distinguished people were his weekend guests.

On November 4, 1927, King George V was a guest at Putteridge for a shoot in the village and the Park. The King, accompanied by Sir

Felix, the Earl of Clarendon, Col. W. Ashley, Col. Jenkins and others bagged 1,001 pheasant, four hares, three rabbits, and six pigeons. On this day all woods in the Park were driven into Audley Dell, where Squire Thomas George had all the high birds. The beaters were village men who wore white coats and red caps. Janet Titmuss was proud of the time when she met King George V. It was at the time of the above shoot that the King was walking down the Allotments Lane carrying his shooting stick. Janet was standing with a neighbour in Saunders Yard, and when she saw His Majesty walking towards them she dropped him a curtsey, which he acknowledged with a "Good morning" and went on to ask her various questions. Janet chatted to the King for quite some time.

Admiral Fisher came on November 26, when only 152 pheasant were shot. A guest on December 20 was the Earl of Verulam for a shoot in the Park, the swag being 327 pheasant and two wild duck; eight more being shot on January 14, 1928, also in the Park. A farmers' shoot four days later got only one pheasant, but shot 108 hares.

On November 27, 1929, in weather described by gamekeeper Herby Gower as "splendid", His Royal Highness the then Duke of York, Sir Felix Cassel, Sir Harry Stonor, Sir Samuel Hoare, Lord Ineagh, Capt. C. Reid and Mr. R. Cain bagged in the village 1,292 pheasant, three partridge, twenty-six hares, three rabbits, one pigeon and one woodcock.

The village now has a thriving football and cricket team, but that is all. In the 1920's, however, the story was much different. Then, there were two hockey teams — ladies' and mixed — both playing at Putteridge Park. In addition to hockey, there were also at this time two football and two cricket teams, and a Lilley Sports Club, which met nightly in the old Victory Hall, where members could enjoy all the usual indoor games plus a game of tennis in the summer.

Village cricket is a tradition as old as the game itself. The healthy and heart-warming "thwack" of willow against leather could be heard from the vicinity of the Lilley Arms on the Saturdays that the village team was at home. Its ground then, the early part of the twentieth century, was the meadow belonging to the inn, which made a beautiful setting for a village cricket match, but not as perfect, some would say, as Putteridge Park, which was the club's ground in 1895. A fixture card for that year reveals that Squire Thomas George was the president with G.B. Hudson, MP, F.W. Fellowes, F.H.A. Sowerby, H.J. Sowerby, E.A. Haviland and R.H. Haviland as vice-presidents. The treasurer was E. Trussell, secretary O. Bodsworth and committee C. Stillwell, H. Trussell, V. Hawkins, H. Payne, W. Toyer and W. Attwood. Fixtures commenced on June 1 and ended on August 31, and were against King's Walden, Caddington, Whitwell, Kimpton, Silsoe, Luton St. Matthew's, and were then repeated to the end of the season.

The star of the side after the First World War was without doubt the late Charles Toyer. He was a useful bowler and an excellent batsman, often "carrying his bat" through an innings. In one game with Hexton, always a "needle" match, he had scored about thirty and was getting set for a big score, when he was given out for picking up the ball and throwing it back to the bowler. Technically, the umpire was correct, but Lilley never forgave Hexton for this, accusing them of conspiring to get rid of Charles.

On this ground, Ernie Payne once played for three seasons without missing a game, and Squire Thomas George was such a good batsman that very often he would place a shilling on the bails, and challenge anyone to knock it off while he was at the crease, the shilling piece being the prize. It was not often that he was twelve pennies worse off! Others who played for the team at this time were H. Attwood, E. Strudwick, J. King, C. Dell, W. Stevens, H. Bavister, W. Fossey, C. Bland, W. Chapman and Alf Wilson. For away games the team travelled in a horse-drawn brake.

Later, the team moved to the recreation ground (which had been given to the village by Thomas Meadows Clutterbuck) and then to Putteridge Park again, at the invitation of Sir Felix Cassel, a benefactor to the people of Lilley who, towards the end of his life, gave the village £5,000 for a new village hall. The ground at Putteridge was in a delightful setting, and Sir Felix used to be a regular visitor, carrying his canvas armchair from the mansion. On some Bank Holidays he would supply the two teams with lunch. Teas were always noticeable for their salad content — freshly cut lettuce and tomatoes from the nursery.

Social activities were an annual dinner held at the Victory Hall, when the best bowler and batsman were presented with a ten shilling note donated by the squire. Ted Holmes once won best bowler award for three consecutive years. After each game at Putteridge the majority of players used to assemble in the Silver Lion, where a very generous helping of bread, cheese and pickled onions was the prelude to a few hours of dominoes and darts, and

An old photograph of Lilley village cricket club 'doing it proud' at Putteridge Park. MT

Some members of Lilley Cricket Club in the early 1900s, posing in Putteridge Park. PC

all well garnished with pints of mild and bitter. The local "derby" now was the match against Offley, and some very hard-fought games ensued. Another highlight was an all-day game with Clophill on August Monday. Umpires were John Boddy and Phil Titmuss, Fred Holmes and "Pete" Taylor at different times.

It would be invidious to single anyone out for special mention in the latter years of the club's history, for many and varied were the club's supporters. It is good that the village, after a lapse of many years, once again has a cricket club, but perhaps sad that the many fine traditions of the past, and the many fine players have now been forgotten.

Chapter 12

Some Famous Common Land

Lilley Hoo. What effect do these words have upon us? Some, no doubt, remember a pleasant heath, the birds singing among the leafy branches, rabbits scurrying here and there on their own mysterious business, wild flowers bowing to a gentle summer breeze or holding up their heads defiantly to a blazing sun, the sheep tugging intently at the short grass; the whole encompassed in the glory and wonder of nature. Some think of it as part of our heritage from Medieval times. Yet others feel resentment or anger that it is not the place it used to be, since it was ploughed and cultivated.

I suppose the latter is the most common feeling of village folk; and yet are we right to feel like this? Is there any proof that the Hoo is a relic of the waste or common land of long ago? On the other hand, is there any proof that it is not?

It is not the purpose of this book to try to prove or disprove any theories regarding the Hoo, but merely to relate what I have discovered from old documents and history books, and leaving you, the reader, to draw what conclusions you like. There are some no doubt, who have discovered more than I. To their greater knowledge, I humbly bow.

In "The Story of a Small Village" Hibbert, in writing of the enclosure, states that Lilley Hoo was not dealt with and that nothing was said of the rights of common there.

I suggest it was not enclosed because it was used as a racecourse. Patronised by nobility far and near, it is unlikely that they would agree to have their favourite pastime spoilt, even by Parliament, and in fact, further weight is added to this theory by the particular Enclosure Act relating to Lilley, which allowed common land to be enclosed, "except a certain sheepdown called Lilly Hoo".

Earlier in his book Hibbert says that the Hoo remains to show us what the "waste" was like.

As far as I have been able to ascertain, Lilley's "waste" or "common" was land lying around Lilley Park Wood, although there could have been "waste" land to the east as well, but historians do not mention specifically that there was. Except for calling the Hoo a "common" they make no further reference to it. Conversely, the "Customs of the Manor of Lilley", a 400-year-old document, which I have examined in some detail, states quite categorically that only sheep could be grazed on the Hoo; that no one had the right to cut down trees or draw firewood, and that tenants did so on pain of a fine.

Whether the Lord of the Manor, who drew up these rules, had any legal right to include the Hoo is not for me to say.

Sir Henry Chauncy, writing in his "Historical Antiquities of Hertfordshire" about the village, states: "This village received the addition of Hoo to its name from that ancient family of the Hoos, who in old time were possessors hereof and in the reign of Edward I Robert d'Hoo, whose chief seat was at Hoo in the County of Bedford, was Lord of this Mannor". He goes on: "Sir Thomas Hoo, who was created and installed Knight of the Garter by Henry VII, unfortunately begat only four daughters, when upon his death, his estate passed to Thomas Hoo, Esq., who sold Lilley in the time of Henry VIII to Lord Vaux of Harrowden". So says Chauncy, but Robert Clutterbuck, in his County history, says this is totally unfounded and that the Hoos never at any time had possession of this Manor.

It is evident from other sources that Clutterbuck was right. The Hoos did not own the Manor of Lilley, but Thomas Hoo did own land here, the last remnant of his estate, which he sold to Lord Vaux of Harrowden. Is it possible this land was what we now call Lilley Hoo, and that this was how it got its name?

On May 26, 1863, Col. Thomas Sowerby brought an action against a Mr Sworder for a trespass on Lilley Hoo. There was a settlement out of court, Mr Sworder admitting he had no defence in the matter. The copy of the settlement says: "In the Exchequer. Sowerby v Sworder. Colonel Sowerby having brought an Action against Mr Sworder, It is admitted and agreed that the cause of Action was for a trespass committed by Mr Sworder with other persons on a Common called Lilley Hoo in the parish of Lilley in the County of Hertford by holding certain Races there on the eleventh day of December last. Colonel Sowerby claims and Mr Sworder admits that Lilley Hoo is a Common within the Manor of Lilley and that it is in Colonel Sowerby's possession as Lord of the said Manor. Mr Sworder consents to pay the costs of the action and the sum of one shilling by way of acknowledgement and amends for such trespass which Colonel Sowerby agrees to accept".

And now for more pleasant things. P.G. Bond, in his "Rambles

Around Luton", talks about the dew pond on the Hoo, and says: "A theory has been advanced that many ancient British camps relied upon them for water, and it seems rather more than a coincidence that close to this dew pond, where the footpath across the Hoo meets the top of Telegraph Hill, is an interesting earthwork, which has actually been identified as one of these early camps. Although the present dew pond has been constructed comparatively recently it is possible that the adaptability of the hill for making one led the Britons to camp here".

The Place Names Society volume for Hertfordshire, states: "Telegraph Hill. Spot suitable for a beacon fire to pass on certain expected news". Of the Royalist and Roundhead days we read: "One after another the fires of Wendover, Ivinghoe, Totternhoe and Lilley Hoo flashed news of the King's approach". The king was Charles I approaching Hertfordshire with an army of 10,000.

Rupert Brooke, the poet, who died in the First World War, knew the Hoo well. Here he would walk while at Cambridge University by:

> The Roman Road to Wendover,
> By Tring and Lilley Hoo.

His route, of course, was the Icknield Way (something else for which the Hoo is noted), which forms the village's northern boundary, and is famous, among other things, for its memories of Queen Boadicea and her East Anglian Iceni tribe. Boadicea is reputed to have travelled this route when marching to fight the Romans, heading thousands of her followers towards the site of a terrible battle, the situation of which has caused a deal of disagreement among historians.

The approach to the Icknield Way from the South, that is over the Hoo, provided at one time some of the loveliest scenery to be found in the whole of Hertfordshire. Here it was possible to lose oneself among shrubs and trees, woods and spinneys; along sheep tracks and broad walks. One was able to find here, too, an abundance of wild flowers, blackberries and crab apples, but let P.G. Bond have the last say: "To the left the thickets are so close that the twittering of the birds in their midst is plainly audible, but later on the path takes its course more centrally, so that in parts it seems that one is walking over a heath, and such a pleasant heath that only England can boast. At the end of this delightful path I felt an irresistable desire to return just for the pleasure of walking over it again".

It seems a pity that we today cannot describe the Hoo like this, doesn't it?

Chapter 13

The Sport Of Kings

It is not generally known, I should think, that Lilley Hoo once boasted a famous racecourse. But it did, and its fame spread far and wide — until the end of the eighteenth century that is, when the meetings mysteriously ceased.

It must have been quite an event for our forbears to witness the arrival of nobility in their fine clothes; the bookmakers and other hangers-on; the grooms and stable lads, and the horses, as they made their way to the Hoo.

Evidence of the races first comes to light in an issue of "The London Gazette", dated September 7/12, 1693:

> "There is a plate to be run for worth £30 on Michaelmas Day next on Lilly Hoo in Hertfordshire; three heats by hunters that never ran for any plate or match before September last, 1692; the winning horse to be sold for £40. Each stranger to put in £5 which is to be stakes for the second horse and to be entered at the George Inn at Silsoe the morning before the said Plate is run for."

Such was the start of Lilley Hoo Races. Of the founders and instigators we know nothing, and it is a pity their names have not survived, for very little information is available about horse racing at this time.

There have been horse races for many centuries. They were known to have been run in the re-establishment of the Olympic Games in 884. In this same century a present of "running horses" was sent by Hugh, founder of the royal house of Capet, in France, to King Athelston the Saxon king, whose sister, Ethelswitha, he was soliciting in marriage.

In the reign of William the Conqueror, Roger de Bellesme, afterwards Earl of Shrewsbury, had some stallions brought from Spain, and James Christie Whyte in his "History of the English Turf", was of the opinion that this was the first well-attested step we can find towards the improvement of this breed of horses.

When Henry II was monarch, horse races began to be frequent exhibitions; and Smithfield was the venue for these early meetings.

While Richard the Lionheart was on his crusades, the popularity of racing in this country was very great. Sir Bevys of Stampton describes the sports in the Easter and Whitsuntide holidays thus:

> In somer time at Whitsontyde,
> When knights, most on horsebacke ryde;
> A courselet they make on a daye,
> Steedes and polfraye, for to assaye;
> Which horse, the best may run,
> Three myles the course was then,
> Who might ryde him should
> Stave forty pounds of redy gold.

Elizabeth I maintained a stud and two jockeys at Hampton Court, and regular meetings began at Newmarket in the reign of James I (1605-25), and either in his reign or that of Charles II two regular meetings were established there in spring and autumn. There were no professional jockeys, gentlemen riding their own horses; the meetings consisted mainly of matches and results were not published.

In 1693, apart from Newmarket and Lilley Hoo, there were also race meetings at Durham, Farringdon, Quainton, Woburn, Stapleton and Ripon. The following year a meeting was established at Blandford, the Salisbury fixture was revived and year by year there were additions to the list with an increasing number of heat races as a variation to matches, and these were the type of events to be witnessed upon the Hoo.

The first meeting at Lilley was a great success and was repeated the following year, when a new inn appears to have been built somewhere in the village, for a notice stated that horses should be entered under the sign of "The Running Horse" at Lilley.

The Transactions of the East Herts Archeological Society tell us that "the inn at Lilley Hoo was appropriately called 'The Running Horse'". But was it located at Lilley Hoo?

Apart from the previously mentioned statement no evidence exists to tell us more, but there are two other possibilities which to me, are much more acceptable! (1) That the present "Lilley Arms", alias "The Sowerby Arms", alias "The Sugar Loaf", dating, as far as is known, from 1705, had yet a fourth name — "The Running Horse", dating from 1694 or (2) that the inn was located at the Flints, which could then have been part of the Hoo.

The meeting continued to be a success and the date was moved forward earlier into September, until in 1697 the date of the meeting was for the first Wednesday in September.

The following year is particularly interesting in that the "Articles Agreed Upon" for that and subsequent meetings were published and are still in existence in the British Museum (Add. MS 28,093). As articles for race meetings of this period are exceedingly rare, a full copy will not be out of place, and, I hope, will be of interest:

> Articles agreed upon this seventh day of September Anno Dom 1698, for a plate to be run for yearly for the space of three years upon Lilly Hoo in the County of Hertford:
>
> 1 Imprimis. It is agreed that any horse, mare or gelding may run for this plate that never ran for above fifty pounds in plate or match.
>
> 2 It is agreed that every horse, mare or gelding that runs for this plate shall carry ten stone weight with bridle, saddle and one pound shall be allowed for wasting every heat.
>
> 3 It is agreed that every horse, mare or gelding that shall be intended to be run for this plate shall be shown and entered at the signe of The Running Horse in Lilly a weeke before the day appointed for the race any time before sunsett.
>
> 4 It is agreed that every horse, mare or gelding that runs for this plate shall start at the Starting Post in Lilly Hoo betwixt the hours of one and three of the clock and run the three heats, four miles each heat, as the same are marked out on Lilly Hoo, leaving all posts and flags on the left hand saving one flag standing or to be placed as usually near the two posts by the corner and that only shall be left on the right hand and half an hour shall be allowed for rubbing betwixt each heat.
>
> 5 For the providing of this plate and ordering the course it is agreed that Henry Sykes shall be Clerke of the Course for the space of three years, and it is severally agreed by us whose names are subscribed and we do hereby promise to pay unto the said Henry Sykes the severall and respective sums hereunder subscribed

yearly at demand during the said three years and in case failure shall happen to be made of any of the said respective payments that then we the said subscribers doe agree that every subscriber soe neglecting to pay the same shall forfeit to the said Henry Sykes the sum of five pounds out of which respective sums he may lawfully deduct the sum of forty shillings for his paynes and trouble.

6 It is agreed that the owner of the winning horse, mare or gelding shall give to the Clerke of the Race twenty shillings upon delivery of the plate.

7 It is agreed that if any subscriber enters a horse, mare or gelding to run for this plate in any of the three years he shall make his subscription money every year forty shillings as well that year he shall run a horse that there may be no inequality in the subscriptions.

8 It is agreed that the moneys paid unto the Clerke of the Course over and above the sums hereunder subscribed shall go towards the bettering of the plate the ensueing year and over incident extraordinary charges.

9 It is agreed that no subscriber shall enter more than one horse, mare or gelding as a founder.

10 It is agreed that if any horse, mare or gelding fairly entered wins two heats together and saves distance the third such horse, mare or gelding shall be adjudged to win the Plate and the owner of such horse, mare or gelding may receive it or any other person for such owner.

11 It is agreed that if three severell horses, mares or geldings win three severell heats a fourth heat must be run and the horse, mare or gelding that wins that heat shall be adjudged to have won the Plate, and it may be delivered to the owner of such horse, mare or gelding or to any other person for the use of such owner.

12 It is agreed that the owner of the winning horse, mare or gelding or some other sufficient person for such owner notwithstanding the two articles above mentioned for the delivery of the Plate shall enter into a Bond before the delivery of the Plate if required of the Penalty of one hundred pounds for the payment of fifty pounds to the owner of the horse, mare or gelding that shall come second to the ending post and five pounds to

the Clerke of the Race in case such horse, mare or gelding shall have run for above fifty pounds in Plate or Match, and if such Bond shall be refused to be entered into then it shall be lawful for the Clerke of the Course to deliver the plate to the owner of such horse, mare or gelding that come next best for the Plate who is hereby adjudged and declared to have won it, and if a Bond be entered into the same together with a Warrant of Attorney to put it in Suite, shall be left in the hands of the Clerke of the Course.

13 It is agreed that the Clerke of the Course shall keepe a Booke wherein shall be fairly entered such moneys as he shall receive and pay, which may be inspected by any subscriber every Race.

14 It is mutually agreed that if any rider strike or take hold of another or show any manner of foul play contrary to the Rules of Newmarkett the horse, mare or gelding that shall soe doe, shall be adjudged to have lost the Plate, and if such foul play be shown the first or second heat, such horse, mare or gelding shall run no more for the Plate.

15 And also it is mutually agreed that if any disputes or controversies doe arise concerning the Plate, riding entrance or race they shall be considered and determined by a majority of the subscribers present.

16 It is agreed that every stranger on the entring day shall pay four pounds and five shillings and every subscriber his subscription money and likewise five shillings for the entring of his horse, to the Clerke of the Course.

The meetings still grew in repute, and in 1699 a start was made with a Spring meeting, for there appeared in "The London Gazette" of March 13/16 1699:

"A Plate of £20 value to be run for on Lilly Hoo in Hertfordshire on Wednesday, the 29th instant, any horse to run that never won above £40 in Plate or money and to carry eleven stone; none but Gentlemen to ride. The horses to be shown and entered the Saturday before at The Running Horse in Lilly where will be a good Ordinary on the Race-day. Likewise a Plate of £5 and a pair of Silver Spurs will be run for."

This Spring meeting, however, was not a success, and it ceased a few years later. In 1710 the date of the race was Thursday, October 12, when a Plate of 20 guineas was run for, and we read that "every horse must be shown at the new stables in Lilly". Which suggests the place was getting to be quite a miniature Newmarket. The stables were located at Lilley Hoo Farm.

Nathaniel Salmon's "History of Hertfordshire", published in 1728, tells us that "The adjunct Hoo is retained for that piece of ground where the Horse race is kept. Here they make a four-mile course of two rounds upon a good turf, but the turnings are too short".

In 1768/9 the enclosure of land came to Lilley but, because of the horse racing, did not include the Hoo, which was then officially described as a sheepdown. By now the race had grown into a three-day meeting and commanded the attention of nobility in Hertfordshire, Bedfordshire and elsewhere.

In 1775 it was held on Tuesday, Wednesday and Thursday, August 8, 9 and 10. The results given in the Racing Calendar were as follows:

> (1) A Subscription Cup of 100 gs value and 30 gs. in specie (coined money as distinct from paper money — Author) for hunters. One four-mile heat. Mr Hale's b.h. Skipjack, 6 years old, 1; Mr Brand's gr. h. Festino, 5 years old, 2; Mr Ledash's gr. h. Teucer, 5 years old, 3.
>
> (2) Same day: £50 given by Sir Benjamin Rawling. Four-mile heats. Sir Chas. Bunbury's b.h. Wolfey, 1. (Sir Benjamin Rawling was owner of Lilley at the time.)
>
> (3) Same day: £50 given by the Stewards. Two-mile heats. Mr Vernon's ch. c. Revenge, 4 years old, 7st. 7 lbs.
>
> (4) The 9th. A Sweepstake of 10 gs. each. Mr Vernon's gr. c. Barbary, 4 year old, 1; Sir Chas. Bunbury's b. h. Wolfey, 5 years old, 2.
>
> (5) Same day: £50 given by members of the County. Lord March's gr. c. Harbinger, 4 years old, 7 st 5 lb. 1.
>
> (6) Same day: £50 given by Thomas Brand and John Radcliffe. Sir Chas. Bunbury's ro. f. Margaretta, 4 years old, 8 st. 4 lb., 1.
>
> (7) The 10th. Sir Chas. Bunbury's b. f. Madselle Heinel beat Mr Brand's gr. f. Magnolia, both 3 years old, 7 st 7 lb. each, for 100 gs.

(8) The £50 Give-and-take was not run, for Mr Vernon's Mecca only being entered, was allowed 10 gs.

(9) Same day: £50 for 4-year-olds. Four-mile heats. Sir Chas. Bunbury's b.c. Vagrant by Omnium.

The "Gold Race Cup" for the first race was given by the famous Lady Salisbury, Master of the Hatfield Hunt, and the course stewards were Lord Grimston and the Hon. W. Stewart, and among those running horses were Sir Charles Bunbury, Lady Frances Ratcliffe, Lady Melbourne, the Duke of Devonshire, the Duke of Grafton, Lord Clermont, Lord Milstown and Sir J. Rous.

Other subscribers for Hertfordshire in 1775 were: Mr Atkinson, Mr Bell, Mr Boulton, Crown Inn, Hockrill; T. Brand, Esq., Mr Crisp, Lieut. Gore, Mr Gray, Major Gwyn, Wm Hale Esq., Wm. Higginson, Esq., J. Houblon, Esq., Mr Lord, Mr North, Mr Perrin, Wm. Phillimore, Esq., Mr Salter, Jun., Edw. Sparhauke, Esq., Wm. Spence, Esq., Mr Taylor, Jun., Mr Watson and Mr Wood.

The races were not without incident and on Wednesday, August 9, 1775, John Lord, the proprietor of a drinking booth "upon Lilley Hoo during the races" was robbed while asleep of the whole of his day's takings.

In the County Records, volume II, this statement is somewhat enlarged: "Eleventh August. Information of Thomas Dudley, of Northampton, labourer. That he was in the booth at Lilly Hoo, belonging to John Lord, victualler, on Wednesday last, and continued therein all that evening and the day following. That he saw William Wentworth and James Dean come into the booth and ask for a glass of gin. They then sat down to drink the beer they had brought with them at the table on which was a lighted candle. One of them designedly put out the candle by throwing it down, at which time the said James Dean was sitting by the said John Lord while asleep. That about half-an-hour afterwards the said John Lord awoke and told the informant he had had his pocket picked of a double pocket containing all the money his wife had taken that day.

"Fifteenth August. Information of Martha Lord, wife of John Lord, victualler, of Market Street (now Markyate). That she had a booth upon Lilly Hoo during the races, and on Wednesday afternoon she left the said booth and delivered to her husband a pair of pockets in which was a sum of 40s. and more." There does not appear to be any further reference to the case.

To return to the races, the following year £50 was given by Thomas Brand and John Radcliffe, Esq., and HRH the Duke of Cumberland had a horse entered for the five-year-old race, and in 1777 the races were held in the middle of July. Lord Cranbourn and the Hon. William Grimston being stewards. There was a race between a horse of Sir C. Barnfyldes and one of William Brand's for 200 guineas over a course of one mile.

The last meeting of any consequence to be recorded in "The Racing Calendar" was on July 17 and 18, 1778, three events worth £50 to the winner and three subscription races of £10 each entrant. Mr Vernon won four of these, Mr Walker and Sir J. Rous the other two.

Others who ran horses were Lady Frances Ratcliffe, Lady Melbourne, Sir Charles Bunbury, the Duke of Grafton, Lord Milstown, Lord Clermont, Mr Hale, Mr Smallman, Mr Stevenson and Mr Read.

Why the decline in the popularity of Lilley Hoo Races occurred is not clear. However, some racing could still be seen on the Hoo, because George, heir to the throne and son of George III, often rode in the point-to-point meetings while staying with Emilius Henry Delme, at Highdown, Pirton. Now George IV was born in 1762 and assuming that he was about 20 years old before he took an active interest in horse racing, we have a date of 1782, or thereabouts, when racing on the Hoo was still in evidence.

Taking the matter a little further, in a pencil note to Salmon's "History of Hertfordshire" written by Dr. Patrick Young, sometime Rector of Northchurch, and now in the Bodleian Library, it is stated: "Wm. Stevenson forbade Lilley Hoo Races, and Lord Melbourn transferred them to his park, where a £50 plate is intended by Wm. Hale and others to encourage their horses".

Races were first held at Brocket Hall (the home of Lord Melbourn) in 1799, so we must assume that the last race meeting of sorts on the Hoo was in the previous year, 1798, ten years after John Sowerby became owner of Putteridge Bury and Lilley.

The intriguing questions here, which up to now I have found no answer for, are: Who was Wm. Stevenson? Why did he stop the races? A man called Stevenson ran a horse at Lilley in 1778. Was he the same man? The County Record Office have been unable to help; neither have the available history books. So, for the time being, Wm. Stevenson must remain a mystery.

Chapter 14

The Squires

The Sowerby family's association with Lilley and Putteridge Bury began in 1778, when John Sowerby, a wealthy Hatton Garden merchant, purchased the estate from the relative of Sir Benjamin Rawling, who had died in 1775.

John was born in 1745, son of Joseph Sowerby, of Brownelstone, Cumberland, and was baptised at neighbouring Dalston, on June 17, 1746. His paternal grandfather was a husbandman, also named John, of Dalston Hall. Like Dick Whittington, his grandson decided that London was the place to search for a fortune, and again like Whittington, his adventure paid off, for it has been written that John made a fortune by purchasing at Lloyds a ship and cargo on which the underwriters had already paid out as a total loss. Next morning, it is alleged, the ship sailed into the Thames, and John was a rich man. Whether or not this story is true, I do not know, but he was certainly a wealthy man, for apart from Lilley and Putteridge, he also owned estates in Bedford, Middlesex, Cumberland and Southampton.

John and his wife, Mary, begat sixteen children, ten sons and six daughters. A plaque in the Sowerby Chapel of St. Peter's Church commemorates Mary, who died on June 29, 1812, aged 58. Her husband died eleven years later.

William Sowerby, eldest son, succeeded his father as Squire in 1823. He remained unmarried, and took a particular interest in horse racing, owning a gelding called Coroner.

National racing was going well at this time. The locomotive was being talked about, but it was generally agreed that "The Iron Horse" would be no threat to the four-legged variety. There were sales to attend at Newmarket, Tattersalls of Knightsbridge, and to a lesser extent at Smithfield Horse Market. There were also the big county fairs where horse sales were held, one of the biggest being at Stourbridge, which often disposed of between 3,000 to 4,000 horses annually. If not attending sales, a country gentleman had much to occupy his time, racing at point-to-point meetings, hunting and riding. It was against this background that William Sowerby lived and raced his horses.

In 1829 Coroner won a race at the first Newmarket meeting; won the Burghley Stakes and Gold Cup at Stamford in July, and in August won the Gold Cup at Newport Pagnell. In 1830, he won at Newmarket in May and July; won the Gold Cup at Stamford, and was beaten by a neck for the Oatlands Stakes at Newmarket in October. The following year, he had ten outings, being second for the Crive Stakes at St. Albans; won on the following day at the same meeting, and won the Plate at Newport Pagnell. In 1832, he ran six times, winning at Newmarket in May and the Town Plate at Newport Pagnell. This seems to have been his last competitive season.

William died in 1838, when his brother Thomas became Squire. He, too, was unmarried, and was a Colonel in the Coldstream Guards, fighting under the Duke of Wellington at Waterloo. He died in 1864, when his brother George took over the reigns of estate management.

George Sowerby married Anne Johnson, of Dalton Hall, Yorks, who gave him four children, George, Thomas Charles, Frances Elizabeth and Mary Anne. He was a JP; a Deputy Lieutenant of Hertfordshire and died in 1868.

He was succeeded by his eldest son, George, who was married to Emily Airey, of Jesmond, Newcastle. They had three sons and three daughters: Thomas George, Harry John, Francis Hubert, Emily Frances, Lilian Mary and Violet Florence. George II was a JP and a Colonel in the Durham Militia. He died in tragic circumstances on August 2, 1888, being gored by one of his own deer in Putteridge Park.

An inquest was held at the Park, the Coroner being F. Shillitoe, Esq., of Hitchin. A key witness was a Herbert Sworder, who was with Colonel Sowerby when the attack was made by the deer and who did his best to rescue him from the enraged animal. A report of the inquest tells us that Mr. Sworder was a young man of nineteen or twenty years of age and of slight build. In evidence, he said: I live at Westmill, near Buntingford, with my father. I am now staying at Durham House, Luton. On Thursday I left Luton at five minutes to three o'clock for Putteridge Bury. My cousin, Clara Sworder, drove me over to see Colonel Sowerby to ask his permission to photograph the deer in the park. I had a photographic apparatus with me. We saw Colonel Sowerby in the garden as we drove up. He readily gave the permission asked for, and said he was pleased to see me. He showed us a lot of things in the house and said he hoped we would come again. When we left the house we were going towards the lodge to photograph the deer there, but he wished us to see the foreign deer first. We all three went to the enclosure where the foreign stag was. He turned into the gate, and I was going to follow him, when he said, "Don't come in; you're a stranger", and added, laughing, "Perhaps he may run at me". He said he would move the stag round so that I might have a good view of it.

I turned partly behind a tree to undo my camera. My cousin turned round and said, "Can I help you?" I said, "No". She turned round again and screamed, "Look, he's down". I jumped over the fence into the enclosure calling to her as I did so to run for help; at the same time I shouted as loud as I could. Colonel Sowerby was lying on his back at the time, pinned down by the stag's antlers. There was a gash near his eye. He exclaimed, "All right", and then seemed to become insensible. He was clutching the antlers; I got one hand free and took out my knife. Colonel Sowerby seemed to get fresh life then, and said, "All right, we'll manage him yet". Those were the last words I heard him speak.

The stag bolted back from us, and as it did so I dropped my knife. I called to Colonel Sowerby to get up, but he could not. The stag came at us again. I caught its antlers, slipped under it, and somehow threw myself over its head. I then succeeded in holding it until a man came up. It seemed a long time before he came. Afterwards, two more men came, and we all four threw the stag over the fence of the enclosure. Colonel Sowerby was bleeding very much at this time. He was put in a chair and I helped to carry him into the house. I waited downstairs until I heard all was over.

Eventually, the jury returned a verdict of accidental death.

For some time after Colonel Sowerby's death, his widow occupied Putteridge Grange and the mansion was let to a Mr. Herring. The new Sowerby Squire, Thomas George, moved to Lilley Manor about 1896 after his marriage to Ellen Pryor, of Weston Park, Hitchin. Emily Sowerby died in 1914, and was interred in Lilley churchyard after a service attended by many local people. A newspaper reported: "A respectful tribute, widespread as it was sincere and devoted to the memory of one whose life and character had been an inspiration of gentleness and kindness . . . such was the demonstration of all classes, rich and poor, at the funeral of the late Mrs. Sowerby, which took place at Lilley Church on Saturday afternoon. Although the afternoon was wet, the commodious interior of the noble parish church was crowded, residents from Hitchin and the surrounding villages being numerously represented, while the porch and aisle near the entrance door was also filled by villagers and others unable to get seats.

George and Emily's third son, Lt. Francis Hubert Airey Sowerby, died at Orange River, Kroonstad, South Africa, on April 1, 1901, in the South African War. The following year, on March 9, the west window of St. Peter's Church was dedicated to his memory. A large congregation saw Thomas George Sowerby unveil the window at a service conducted by Rector Haviland which was "Very touching and impressive in its simplicity . . . when there was a large congregation to manifest their sympathy for the bereaved family and high regard for the memory of the deceased officer, who won the hearts of all that knew him".

Thomas George Sowerby, still spoken of today with respect and fondness, apart from being a first-class cricketer and an excellent shot, was also interested in horses and kept a large contingent of hunters. He also owned the first car in the village, a Buick. He died in 1938.

Thomas George had two sons, Richard Thomas and Hubert Denison, both inheriting their father's interest in cricket and shooting. The late Hubert (or "Pip" as he was called) took an almost fanatical interest in the village cricket club and with such stalwarts as Charles Toyer, Alf Hatton, Stan Payne, Frank Muddle, Jim Nightingale, Ron Claridge, Will James and George and Jim Oliver did as much as was humanly possible to keep the original club going for as long as it did.

In 1908 the house at Putteridge Park was pulled down by a new owner, T.M. Clutterbuck, and remodelled in the Elizabethan style by the architects Sir Ernest George and Yates, who completed the work in 1911.

The family of Clutterbuck is descended from Richard Clutterbuck, a possible immigrant from the Netherlands, who died in 1591. His sons were clothiers at Kings Langley, in Hertfordshire. Sir Thomas, an alderman of London, was the grandson of one of them, and was knighted in 1669.

At the installation of the Duke of Portland, in 1792, as Chancellor of Exeter University, a Thomas Clutterbuck was among those who recited Latin verses composed in honour of the occasion. In 1823, Robert Clutterbuck, BA, FSA, a deputy lieutenant of Hertfordshire and magistrate for Hertford, and the author of a rather austere history of Hertfordshire, was called upon to give evidence in the case of John Thurtell and his accomplices, the murderers of

William Weare, which attracted the interest of the whole country.

Robert Clutterbuck was a Fellow of the Society of Antiquaries, and for eighteen years was busily engaged in the compilation of a new history of Hertfordshire, which, compared with Chauncy, who was before him, and who was witty and gossipy, appeared to be rather austere, but is, nonetheless, a valuable source of information. The work appeared under the title of "The History and Antiquities of the County of Hertford" and was compiled from the best printed authorities and original records preserved in public repositories and private collections. Published in three volumes, 1815, 1821 and 1827, it is claimed that the plates have never been surpassed in any publication. Several of them were from his own sketches and he also secured the assistance of Edward Blare and other eminent draughtsmen and engravers.

While Putteridge was being built the Clutterbucks were the tenants at Chequers, on which house Putteridge is styled. The whole estate was covered in drains, for being on high ground, plants and trees were stunted in growth and late in maturing. A huge underground icehouse was built between the trees, which was kept full of meat, being the only means then of refrigeration. The story is told of the time when all the hounds in full cry after a fox fell into this well and perished. Poetic justice, perhaps?

During the 1914-18 war Mrs Clutterbuck bought clogs and thick macintoshes for many of her employees' children, and gave their parents coal. Her workers could always depend on warm bowls of soup. The employees liked Thomas Clutterbuck, and several of them came with him from Chequers.

It was while Thomas Clutterbuck was living at Putteridge that he had a laundry built and installed electricity. Until this time the public could walk through the Park, but Thomas made it private land, and had a policeman there who locked the gates at 10 p.m. Also at this time a Witch Elm in the park grew so huge that chains were put on it for safety.

One of his daughters died of appendicitis at seventeen years of age, and another married the Hon. Holland Hibbert, of Leighton Buzzard, who led a Peace Parade through the village at the end of the Great War.

Thomas Clutterbuck lived in his new house for only ten years before he died. He loved the open air and was often seen pottering about his beautiful grounds. He caught pneumonia and died in 1919, because, it is said, he insisted on tending his flowers even in the pouring rain. His widow went to live at Little Offley, which house the family sold in 1966. Nearly all the estate of Putteridge and Lilley was sold to the Crown, and Putteridge was acquired by Sir Felix Cassel.

During the 1920's King George V, Queen Mary and the Prince of Wales were frequent visitors to Putteridge, and it was on December 1, 1926, that the King planted the oak tree on the lawn to the south of the mansion.

Putteridge Bury finally severed its connections with Lilley in 1954 on the death of Sir Felix Cassel, who was a benefactor to the village.

Chapter 15

The Parish Council

Local government has existed in one form or another for centuries, but until the Parish Councils Act of 1894 was in a most chaotic state, with boroughs and county boroughs, aldermen and JPs, villages grouped into Unions — which had been formed from the ancient "Hundreds" — sanitary districts and school board districts, and all with no sort of uniformity whatever.

The Parish Councils Act divided the county areas (outside the boroughs) into urban districts and rural districts, and the old sanitary districts were taken as the basis of the division. The sanitary districts, in fact, were renamed as urban or rural districts of the county. Councils were established in the districts with powers and composition not very different from those of towns, except that they did not include aldermen. The rural districts were naturally the most extensive in area, but the least populous, and in each parish of a rural district a parish council was set up, or in very small places, a parish meeting.

So Lilley formed a parish council, which largely took over the role hitherto performed by the village "Vestry". In the notes that follow I have reported mostly on annual meetings. To deal with all the meetings would need a book containing nothing else.

The first-ever meeting of a parish council in the village was held on Friday, January 4, 1895, in the Reading Room. Present were Matthew Feakes, Thomas Foll, Thomas George Sowerby, Harry John Sowerby, Arthur Toyer and Harry Trussell. Mr. T.G. Sowerby was elected chairman — an office he held almost continuously till 1930 — Mr. Foll, vice-chairman; Mr. James Cain (assistant overseer for the parish) clerk to the council, and Mr. W. Tindall Lucas, of the Hertfordshire Hitchin Bank, treasurer.

The first annual meeting was held on April 22, that same year, following a parish election. At this time councillors held office for only twelve months; nowadays, it is for three years. Mr. T.G. Sowerby was again elected chairman; Mr. Foll, vice-chairman; Mr. A.

Toyer and Mr. C. Young, joint overseers for the parish; Mr. T. Farr, way-warden (a man responsible for the upkeep of roads, such as they were), and Mr. H. Trussell, clerk to the council. Then follows a rather mysterious incident concerning Mr. James Cain. To quote from the minutes:

"Proposed by Mr. H.J. Sowerby, seconded by Mr. T.G. Sowerby, that Mr. J. Cain be elected Assistant Overseer. Mr. H. Trussell then proposed that the salary of the Assistant Overseer be £7 per annum. It was seconded by Mr. Foll. An amendment was then moved by Mr. T.G. Sowerby, seconded by T. Foll, that the salary be £8 per annum. Carried unanimously. Mr. J. Cain declined to undertake the duties of Assistant Overseer at the salary named. He also objected to the Council dealing with his election, stating as a reason that they had not the power. Therefore, the election of Assistant Overseer was adjourned."

You will have noticed that at the first meeting of the council Mr. Cain, who was already assistant overseer, was also appointed clerk to the council. At the first annual meeting he was replaced as clerk by Mr. Trussell, so it looks as if he was being rather petulent at being replaced and cut off his nose to spite his face. The council, however, despite Mr. Cain's objection, certainly had the power to elect overseers and assistant overseers as set out in "Statutory Provisions Controlling Proceedings" in the Local Government Act. Previously it had been the "Vestry" that had appointed overseers. Mr. C. Davis, of Hitchin, applied for, and was given, the position of assistant overseer and collector of the highway rate at an annual salary of £7, but seven years later he, too, fell foul of the council and was asked to resign.

We can get some idea of the cost-of-living in 1897 by entries in the minute book for a meeting held on March 13 that year:

To G.A. Passingham for expenses of poll, etc. £9 2s. 3d. (Today, it would cost at least a penny rate); To James Cain for supplying chairs and forms for parish meeting, 15s.; To Albert Toyer for iron grating to drain, 2s.; To H. Trussell (clerk) for stamps and paper, receipt and payment book, etc., £1 2s. In addition, the caretaker of the Reading Room was paid 2s. 6d. for his past services; a footpath across the Green to the Chapel cost £3 6s. 4d.; Mr. Powdrill, material and carting, £2 5s. 4d.; J. Cain for cartage, 9s.; Titmuss for labour, 12s. A meeting on April 29 discussed ways of celebrating the Diamond Jubilee of Queen Victoria, and it was agreed that "a good meat tea would be most appreciated by the villagers". A sign of the times, perhaps?

At the annual meeting on April 21, 1899, James Cain came into favour again when he was elected a joint overseer with Arthur Toyer; and Mr. C. Davis, as assistant overseer, asked for an increase in his salary. The council hedged round this one by holding it over to the next meeting.

At this meeting the question was again postponed until the re-election of assistant overseer. On March 12, 1901, Mr. Davis was again discussed. This time he wanted some remuneration for assisting in the making of a new valuation list. The council, however, took exception to this latest demand and he was requested to attend the next meeting to explain himself, but he did not do so, and the minutes state that "no action was taken on his letter read at the previous meeting". On March 14, 1902, a letter was read from the Finance Committee of the Board of Guardians concerning Mr. Davis's conduct as assistant overseer, so it would appear that he had been getting up to some hanky-panky that is not recorded by the Parish Council.

As a result of this letter he was asked to resign and deliver up all books, etc. to the overseers at once. This he did not do, and the chairman offered to write to the Local Government Board asking its advice. The outcome is not recorded, but the name of C. Davis does not appear again.

Mr. C. Sharp, of Offley, was appointed assistant overseer at £7 per annum, and Francis Allingham appears on the scene for the first time when he was appointed an overseer.

At the meeting of July 25, 1903, the poor old local Press — that grand British institution without which our way of life would be that much poorer — received some criticism from Mr. R. Osborne for remarks contained in the Luton papers about the footpaths across his fields, and he asked the council to take some action. Whether it did so is not made clear, but at the next annual meeting Mr. Osborne resigned. From this we can, perhaps, draw our own conclusions!

The telephone (or telegraph, as it was called) was first mentioned at a meeting on April 20, 1905, when it was decided that the chairman would find out more about it and report to the next meeting. This subject was not discussed again until 1912. Public bodies nowadays are often accused of being long-winded, but seven years, whew! Anyhow, eventually it was decided that Mr. Toyer should see Mr. Robert Farr and others about being guarantors for a telephone service. The GPO was not going to risk a loss!

A special meeting was called on December 23, 1913, for the

purpose of discussing the telephone. According to the minutes the first question put was "Shall we have a telephone?" The meeting agreed to have one installed in the village after Major T.G. Sowerby said he would stand as a guarantor for three-quarters of the amount required, the remaining quarter being found by Francis Allingham, Bert Facer, Arthur Toyer and William Conner. The telephone arrived in due course and in its first year incurred a loss of nearly £6 — a sum met by Major Sowerby. Obviously, villagers didn't take too kindly to the darned thing.

The need for a recreation ground was mooted on April 9, 1914, when the clerk was instructed to write to T.M. Clutterbuck, Esq., with the information that it was the general wish that a recreation ground be provided for the village, and could he kindly help in the matter. On June 12 the council learned that Mr. Clutterbuck was willing to rent four acres opposite Lilley House to the council at £1 per acre per annum, and was willing to provide fencing and a gated entrance in Church Lane.

August 22, 1914, saw the council discussing what action it would take to collect money for the War Relief Fund. A committee was set up, consisting of Major and Mrs. T.G. Sowerby, Esther Cundall, Matthew Feakes, Arthur Toyer, William Conner and John Sansom (clerk), and it was agreed that no canvassing would take place, that notices advertising the fund would be displayed in conspicuous places, and that Mrs. Sowerby and Miss Cundall would receive donations, the first of which amounted to £7 1s. 6d. Also an offertory was taken in church by the Rev. G.H. Genge.

After the Great War, a letter was read to the council on Tuesday, July 8, 1919, from Septimus J. Beck, on behalf of Mr. Clutterbuck, offering a piece of ground to the council to commemorate the Armistice, with the clause that it should be used in perpetuity as a recreation ground, which so far it has been.

As a result of a letter from Hertfordshire County Council, a discussion arose at a meeting on July 19, 1921, on which ponds in the village were publicly owned. The County Council had suggested that the summer drought was perhaps a good time to clean out village ponds. Major Sowerby informed members of the council that the only public one was that opposite the Rectory. Mr. A. Darby of Church Farm, was then directed to employ three out-of-work men to clean it out at seven shillings each per day, which I assume was done. Until searching through the first minute book of the parish council, I had not realised that Doozley Pond *was* publicly owned.

During 1924, Hertfordshire County Council decided to adopt the terms of the Public Libraries Act, and Lilley Parish Council was asked to appoint a honorary librarian and a small library committee. The library was held in the Reading Room weekly, thus giving villagers the opportunity of broadening their outlook, and an excuse, no doubt, to linger in the Reading Room for a bit of a natter.

Chapter 16

Village Characters

Most villages have had, and some still have, inhabitants who could be classed as "characters", and Lilley is no exception. Those in the past were sometimes eccentric, or funny, or lovable, or quaint in their dress. Some were well known for their work or public service; yet others merely for their nicknames.

I suppose it would be true to say that everyone is a "character"; each is an individual with peculiar gifts, peculiar traits, that may annoy or endear them to others, that may even make them immortal, or, as in so many cases, just pass through life completely unnoticed, like so many cabbages in a patch . . . uniform in size and type, and unable to be anything else; they die, they are forgotten — "ashes to ashes, dust to dust".

Even though they have passed through the "vasty hall of death", the people of this chapter are still alive in our memories. Materialising like spectres from the shrouds of the past, they emerge from their home in that part of our sub-conscious that acts as a personal filing cabinet. "Ah", we say, "remember old so-and-so? He used to . . . " And then follows the particular action, statement, work or what-have-you for which so-and-so is remembered.

It will be realised that more than those mentioned here have earned this form of immortality. For their omission I must seek your pardon and indulgence. So let us recall:

Lizzie Martin, badly crippled with arthritis in later life. She helped deliver babies and "lay out" those who had died. It has never ceased to amaze me that nearly every village could produce such women as Lizzie. Whatever the time, day or night, there they were, sleeves rolled up; kind, efficient and firm. Two other women like Lizzie spring to mind: the late Harriet Hulatt (nee Bland) and Daisy Rowe. Doubtless there have been others.

Jane Cain, who walked daily to Luton and treadled a hat machine all day till she was 72. Not very outstanding, you might say. Many other women must have done as much, or more. But Jane is remembered, perhaps for her sheer determination, in her old age, not to be a burden to the parish poor rate.

Susan Bland, church verger for many years, stoking the fire, lighting and trimming the lamps, cleaning and also, it is said, being a great comfort in the course of her duties to the bereaved. What person could wish for a better epitaph? To be able to comfort another in distress is a God-given gift. For some years she worked at Putteridge Mansion scrubbing the laundry floor from 6.30 a.m. to 5 p.m. for 1s. 6d. a day. Prior to this, Susan and her husband Sam had been caretakers at Putteridge. In later life she invariably helped at the dances held there, walking home at two in the morning. On one such occasion, when walking past the church on a moonlit night, she saw in the churchyard a white and eerie shape. I suppose most people would have taken to their heels and ran, but not Susan. She went to investigate, and found a white cat!

Hannah Brown, a kindly soul, who partook of her breakfast at five in the morning, and her lunch at about nine or ten o'clock because, as she said, "I like to get my meals over". Can she be blamed for this? What woman at some time has not wished that all meals were over by lunch-time; all washing-up finished, and she could then, perhaps, relax a little?

George Bean, a member of Lilley Church choir for over fifty years. People I have spoken to say they cannot remember him ever missing a service.

Granny Bland, who kept a small shop. When serving sweets to a customer, she would say, "A quick ha-porth is better than a slow pen'orth". More often than not, children were given sweets; she is said to have been very kind and generous.

Roadmen are a thing of the past now — the last one in Lilley was the ever-popular George Bishop. Before his time, however, one was always to be found in the village. Long, long ago the roadman's name was Payne, "Peggy" they called him, because of his wooden leg. He was a favourite with the children. When they made their way home from school for their lunch they invariabely gathered round him.

One can imagine the scene. A wooden wheelbarrow, a shovel, a broom, a sickle and a rubbing stone. "Peggy" sitting on a bank, perhaps outside the church, eating his bread and cheese, with children around him all talking at once; the scene bathed in sunshine — the church, the trees, the old man, the tools of his trade, and the children. A peaceful scene, a peaceful era; when men had time to think far from the madding crowd. How far have we progressed since, with our constant battle against the clock; with our obsession to keep up with the Jones's and beat the Smiths?

Two village men with a fine reputation were Albert Toyer, "Albert Edward" to his friends, and his son Charles, remembered as Lilley's sub postmaster, churchwarden and Rural District Councillor for many years, and Albert later as a woodman.

In 1917 the Band of Hope was very active in the village. Being a temperance society, many people signed the "pledge". John "Snob" (so called because he was a shoemaker) Sansom sometimes took the meetings, and when he did nearly always lectured on the effects of alcohol on the "blod", as he was wont to call the red and white corpuscles that surge through our veins.

Jabez and Lizzie Cain kept a shop which was in the house now occupied by Emily and Keith Harris. It has been said of Jabez that he was a real old horse dealer; that he bought worn-out London Transport horses, doctored them up in Lilley, and then sold them back to London Transport — at a profit, of course! But whether this story is true, I wouldn't know. Suffice it to say old Jabez was a shrewd businessman.

George Barker was a sawyer. He bought trees which were later cut into planks over a pit, one man on top, another below. It must have taken hours of patient toil to dispose of a tree trunk.

A man renowned for his gentleness, a Wesleyan, was David Coles, a shepherd, like another David who lived thousands of years ago. A photograph of David Coles with his sheep now resides in a building in the USA. It is not for this, however, that he is remembered, but for his love, gentleness and kindness. What dreams, I wonder, were nurtured during the long hours spent alone in the meadows? What secret prayers were invoked to the God whom he served? Was it here that he found his inner strength and peace?

Prior to 1914, two well-known characters were Jim Harry (real name Webb) who always had a short pipe stuck upside down in his mouth, and "Budgie" Clark, the only regular soldier from the village before the Great War. He lived while on leave with his parents behind the old Red Lion, and thrilled children with his tales of heroism. But why was he, do you suppose, called "Budgie"?

Emma Jacob was an old character who, it is said, liked a pint of wallop, and much more than a pinch of snuff. The housekeeping money, however, would not buy enough for Emma, so she "puggled" up her husband's potatoes — that is, she eased them out of the ground without disturbing the plants — and sold them for beer and snuff money. What a shock the poor man must have had when he dug up those plants!

A character often seen around the village in the 1920's and 30's was Sammy Baines, living rough at Ward's Farm. It was his habit, every lunch-time to ride down to the Red Lion on the back of a cart-horse called "Flower". He would leave the horse outside while he went in for a pint, returning a few minutes later with one for "Flower" as well. Sammy would open her mouth and pour down the brown liquid, which the mare drank with as much relish as Sammy did his. Then he would re-mount and ride back to the farm, playing a mouth-organ with much gusto. The story is told of Sammy that when working on a building site the foreman said to him: "Sammy, your mate moves two wheelbarrows to your one". Replied Sammy: "Aye, he did yesterday as well!" It is said that one day he met Alf Payne. After greeting one another, Sammy said: "Alf, if I was carrying my head under an arm, would you recognise me?" We can only imagine Alf's reply!

Some very well-known Rectors have had charge of Lilley over the years. Two who attained immortality through wielding their pens were Francis Aidan Hibbert and Atherton Knowles. Francis Aidan Hibbert wrote Influence of English Guilds, Chapters In Denstone History, History of Denstone College, Bede — The Seatonian Poem, Monasticism in Staffordshire, The Dissolution of the Monastries, The Denstone Register, (Co-editor) English History, 15th and 16th Centuries, 17th Century and English History, 1066-1832, Story of Denstone and its Church, A Miracle Play, and a book known to us all, The Story of a Small Village. Atherton Knowles was the author of A Textbook of Anglian Services and Music from Tallis to Wesley.

Six people who lived in more recent times shall have a place in this chapter:

Richard James Bland, known in his younger days as "Chauffeur". What words are there that will adequately describe the affection and esteem in which he was held? I feel quite inadequate to attempt such a task. Dick was always full of funny stories about his younger days. One that sticks in my mind is about the time he was asked by Mrs. Clutterbuck at Putteridge Bury to assist in the killing of fowl for the dinner table. Now Dick was new to this game. He watched; it looked easy enough. He got hold of an unfortunate bird and performed the necessary actions on the creature's neck. He plucked it, put it on one side, and forgot about it — until the bird rose shakily to its feet, that is, straightened itself up, gathered together all its strength . . . and ran round the yard as if all the demons in hell were after it. If I remember the story correctly, eventually Dick caught the naked bird and beheaded it!

Agnes Gentry. Schoolmistress in the village during the war years. What a life she had! Especially when the evacuees from London arrived. She never could control them. Some people are apt to smirk when talking of Agnes. She did a good job, though, in very trying circumstances.

Frank Webb. Village shoemaker for many years. A man who had a deep love for Lilley. A fine craftsman who is sadly missed.

Sir Felix Cassel, Bart, KC. Benefactor extraordinary to the village. Towards the end of his life he gave £5,000 for a new village hall to commemorate his wife, Lady Helen Cassel.

Jim Nightingale. Stricken with arthritis in the prime of life, but nevertheless always cheerful, and always more than ready to talk about the Lilley sporting scene.

John Boddy, a village Special Constable, with a deep love of the village, always ready to talk about his memories. George Brown and Will Oliver are two more that must be named here. Both lovers and upholders of village life.

We have much for which to thank Matthew Feakes, particularly for his description of the old church at Lilley. A letter of his to Dora Haviland in 1917 is also interesting (though not, of course, so important) for it gives us some idea of the changes that had taken place in the village during the Great War, and names some of its worthies. He writes:

"A good number of our Lilley boys have gone, some have returned wounded and some have lost limbs and are no more fit. We have had many changes at Lilley during the past year. The Trussells have all left the village. The shop and cottage are at present unlet; bread is brought to the village by motor from Luton.

"We have strangers at the Post Office. Arthur Toyer has turned the Church Farm over to a man by the name of Allanson, who married his daughter Annie. He has been at the front and came home minus a leg. Toyer lives on with them.

"Albert Toyer has given up the blacksmiths' work and turned woodman, and a new man is at the forge; also at the farm that was Franklin's. There are several empty cottages in the village. We have some soldiers and three interned Austrians working on the farms.

"I do not think there has been any shortage of labour. Most of the Lilley girls are on munition work at Luton, earning high wages."

This was to be the way of life for more and more women in the years to come. Once more life in our villages, perhaps much more than in our towns, underwent a drastic change.

A couple of events, both sad in their loss, ended an era in which two people — possibly more than any others we can find in the history of this small place — had changed and moulded village life in Lilley.

Upon the death of the Rev. Arthur Coles Haviland it was written:

"Everyone who knew him had the greatest respect for the Rector. He was ever kind to the poor, and the poor appreciated to the full all the efforts he put forth on their behalf. From the youngest to the oldest there was an entire agreement on the point — all felt that they had lost a friend. It may not be general to find such an amicable spirit prevailing in these days of religious differences, but that such existed at Lilley during the life-time of the late Rector, no one will deny. To the members of all denominations he was equally dear, and more than one villager expressed the opinion that they would never see his equal again. That is surely the highest testimonial to a clergyman's work that anyone could obtain. He loved and was loved."

And upon Esther Cundall's death:

"By the passing of Miss Esther Cundall, at the advanced age of 84, Lilley has lost one of its most honoured and respected inhabitants . . . Miss Cundall went to Lilley in 1873, having been appointed head teacher of the National Schools by the late Rector, the Rev. A.C. Haviland. It is difficult to exaggerate the profound respect, affection and admiration in which she had ever since been held by the successive generations of her children. The school flourished exceedingly under her very firm and sympathetic rule; and the nature of her life's work there is best summarised in the following resolution which was unanimously passed by the Managers on her retirement in May, 1908: 'That a hearty vote of thanks be given to Miss Cundall in acknowledgement of the conspicuous ability, zeal and fidelity with which she has discharged the duties of her office during the long period of 35 years. It is felt that words could but inadequately express what is due to her for her work, and the heartiest good wishes are felt for her future happiness and prosperity.'

"Miss Cundall's activities did not cease with her retirement. There was no church or village interest into which she did not largely enter. She became a Manager of the Schools and as such her long experience was much valued. Her presence and advice were ever welcome, and energy in good works was unceasing. It was while on one such work of mercy that ten years ago she slipped and broke a thigh, an accident which had ever since kept her at home. Still her personality continued to hold its sway, and many people found their way to her cottage, going, doubtless, to help cheer her up, but coming away equally cheered and gladdened. Her greatest interest of all was missionary work and, in particular, that of the Lebombo Diocese in South Africa, in which one of the Mission clergy is the Rev. David Trussell, an old pupil of hers at Lilley School.

"Unselfishness and simple, childlike faith were the guiding stars of a long and deeply honoured life, and the intense affection and deep esteem in which Miss Cundall was held prove clearly that these are the things that still really count."

Indeed they are.

In the early years of the 19th century there came to reside in the village a mysterious character called Johan Kellerman. In William Hone's Year Book for 1832 there is an account of this eventual recluse, who took up his residence in a large house (no longer in existence) in the centre of the village. He had not always been a recluse, however.

A Vestry minute book of 1818 reveals: "At a meeting held in the Sugar Loaf in this parish by the principal inhabitants, the following resolution was agreed to ... "Resolved that Mr Kellerman has agreed to pay into the hands of the Overseer of this parish the sum of £50 for an illegitimate child."

He attracted further attention when he shut himself off from the outside world by barricading the house and protecting the walls of the grounds with hurdles and spring-guns, so placed as to resist intrusion from every direction. The shutters were kept tightly closed and Kellerman himself was never seen out. A small gang of local men were employed in an outhouse, constantly blowing an enormous and mysterious pair of bellows. For some years this student of pseudo-chemistry remained at Lilley but disappeared in the same mysterious manner as he had arrived. It is thought he may have fled to Paris, where he had relatives, and in which city he may eventually have died.

It is stated in Hone's Year Book that Kellerman had been a man of fashion and concerned in adventures on the turf, but had withdrawn from his gay life to devote himself to the study of alchemy and philosophical chemistry. From alchemy the modern science of chemistry has evolved, but ancient and medieval alchemy was a semi-occult science, whose goal was the transmutation of base metals into gold, and similar magical projects.

Sir Richard Phillips, in "A Personal Tour through the United Kingdom", has left an account of a visit to Kellerman in the summer of 1828. When staying at Luton he was informed of our recluse who disliked the presence of strangers, and forthwith decided that at all costs he must obtain personal confirmation of the many strange stories and rumours. His description of the house "did not belie vulgar reports" and he could not help shuddering at seeing the high wall of the respectable premises lined at the top with double tiers of hurdles, and, on driving his chaise to the front of the house, observing the whole in a state of horrid dilapidation. He presented his card to a young man in one of the outbuildings, who took it to the back of the house to his master.

The front windows on the ground floor and upper storeys were entirely closed by inside shutters, much of the glass was broken, and the house appeared deserted and untenanted. Phillips was more than surprised when the young man re-appeared with the request that his master would be pleased to see him. The front door opened and the mysterious Kellerman presented himself. As Sir Richard confessed:

"I lament that I have not the pencil of Hogarth; for a more original figure never was seen. He was about six feet high, and of athletic build; on his head was a white nightcap and his dress consisted of a long greatcoat once green, and he had a sort of jockey waistcoat with three tiers of pockets. His manner was extremely polite and graceful, but my attention was chiefly absorbed by his singular physiognomy. His complexion was deeply sallow, and his eyes large, black and rolling."

The visitor was taken into a large room with a window looking towards the back of the house. The alchemist locked the door behind him, placed the key in his pocket, and conducted his guest to one of two large, sheepskin-covered armchairs. The floor of the room was littered with retorts, crucibles, alembics and various chemical paraphernalia intermingled with many old books piled upon each other, with a sufficient quantity of dust and cobwebs.

Kellerman said that he had studied the works of the ancient alchemists and had succeeded in discovering the key they had so well concealed from the outside world. After suffering many disappointments owing to the ambiguity with which their researches had been described, he had at length succeeded in making gold. He boasted to his visitor that he could make as much of the precious metal as he pleased, even to the extent of paying off the National Debt in the coin of the realm.

Phillips gave Kellerman to think that he fully believed these extravagent statements and requested to be shown samples of the synthetic gold. "Not so", replied Kellerman. "I will show it to no one. I made Lord Liverpool the offer that if he would introduce me to the King I would show it to His Majesty; but Lord Liverpool insolently declined, on the ground that there was no precedent; and I am, therefore, determined that the secret shall die with me. It is true, that in order to avenge myself of such contempt, I made a communication to the French Ambassador, and offered to go to France and transfer to the French government the entire advantages of the discovery; but after deluding me, and shuffling for some time, I found it necessary to treat him with the same contempt as the others."

Phillips sympathised with Kellerman in order to gain his further confidence, and was informed that every court in Europe was aware of the great discoveries he had made, but had arranged between themselves against him, fearing that if any one of them obtained the secret that country would be master of them all.

"The world, sir, is in my hands and my power", boasted Kellerman.

The curious visitor asked him then why he had barricaded himself in and kept himself out of the way of village people. It was not on account of their ignorance or insolence alone, but as a measure of protection against the European governments who were anxious to wrest his secrets from him by fair means or foul, he declared. He had already been fired at twice through the window and three attempts at poisoning him had been made. They believed that he had written a book containing his discoveries, and it was this volume they were after. But to make certain his secrets were not divulged he had burnt and destroyed all his writings, and to guard himself further from the unwelcome attentions of his enemies had fortified his windows with spring-guns and had enough combustible material in his room to wipe out an entire regiment of soldiers if the occasion arose.

Kellerman proceeded to relate how, in order to effect further protection, he lived in one room and permitted no one to enter the house, and that, except the one they were in, all the rooms were locked with patent padlocks and the keyholes sealed.

After leaving Lilley, Phillips overtook a man and enquired what the people of the district thought of the strange philosopher who lived among them. The man told him that he was one of the eight assistants working for Kellerman, who were retained for the purpose of superintending the crucibles, two at a time, relieving each other every six hours; that Mr Kellerman exposed preparations to intense heat for many months at a time, but that all but one of the crucibles had burst and that he had called on him to observe that it contained the true "blacker than black" powder.

The man admitted that no gold had ever been produced and that no mercury had ever been fixed. Further severe disappointments appear to have terminated most of his master's elaborate experiments.

The headline said "The Son of a local Baker. Village Boy who ran a Diocese. Memories of his old Schoolmistress".

The "son" was David Trussell; the "baker" — his father — also David Trussell; the "diocese" Lebombo in Africa, and the "schoolmistress" Esther Cundall. Therein lies a story, unfolded for us in an issue of the Luton News, dated May 10, 1923.

The story opens with a verbatim quote of a remark made by the late Dr Furse, Bishop of St. Albans in 1923, when he addressed a meeting at Luton:

"One of the best clergy I ever had out in Africa was the son of a village baker; and the schoolmistress there, she it was who put into this lad's head the idea of being a missionary, and he stuck to it and went to St. Augustine's and got the best education he could. That fellow in the absence of the Bishop, ran the whole diocese. All due to the schoolmistress. If a small village can produce that, we ought to be producing many more."

So spoke Dr Furse. Thus this small village, famous in history for many things, and breathing still today the air of antiquity, found itself in the proud position of having supplied a text to a most well-known and modern Bishop, and given to many, through David Trussell, born of humble yet noble stock, the words of Eternal Life.

The story continues: "In such 'haunts of ancient peace' men arise who hear a call amid the brooding silences of wood and field and, breaking the bonds that would bind them to the soil, fare forth to greater service and greater fame. Some may find it within the confines of their own land. Some may go beyond."

So ventured David Trussell, son of a baker, a pupil of the village school; once a boy as any other boy, yet even then possessing the spirit of a humble Nazarene carpenter, the Master of all who would call themselves Christian.

We go on: "Although the whole of the other members of his family have died or have left the village, David Trussell remains as something more than a memory with village folk. One who, though now burdened with years, has still the blessing of all her faculties, and remembers him with especial pride and pleasure, is his old schoolmistress."

The story now deals with a visit a reporter made to Esther Cundall:

"Leaving the main road and passing along the winding village street with its houses old and its houses new, its parish church and its memorial of the great sacrifice of the war years, the visitor comes at length to two neat little houses, slightly raised above the roadway, garden ground all about them, bright with flowers and alive with the humming of bees, trees o'er shadowing, and meadows beguiling. The very essence of pastoral peace, it appears — a pleasant spot in which to end one's days. Seated facing the open doorway, through which the soft zephyrs of summer gently steal, sits an elderly lady in a grey dress, with white lace at the throat, matching the snow-white of her hair. Miss Cundall makes the visitor welcome in kindly and gracious manner and readily consents to talk of her late pupil, although she is sorry that she cannot remember more, because her memory is not what it used to be.

"After hearing Dr Furse's tribute to her part in the making of the man and the missioner, Miss Cundall modestly assures the visitor that the Bishop has been altogether too generous in his praise. She, however, admits that she may have played a part in the shaping of David's career.

"Born in the village in a house which has since been demolished, David, the son of David — but so named because he was born on St. David's Day — received his early education at the village school, the fruit of the generosity of a former incumbent, who has left his mark behind in many directions.

"'He was a very bright, intelligent boy and particularly fond of scripture lessons', Miss Cundall recalls. 'The Diocesan Inspector used to praise him very much. He did not tell me that he had the idea of being a missionary, but I think it must have been in his mind a long time, and when he had the opportunity he wished to be trained. He gave me the credit of giving him the idea, but that must have been in his usual lessons. From a child I was interested in missionary work, and I have no doubt a good deal of it came through in my lessons. His whole heart and soul was in the work. He always attended the Sunday School and was in the choir.'

"The future missioner used to pay a visit to Miss Cundall's house occasionally, as some of the village children love to do today."

Our story continues: "David, approaching middle age today, was a member of a large family supported by his father from the proceeds of a bakery business, carried on in premises near the Post Office, and now used as a dwelling house. Whether this proximity to the mails and the stamps had anything to do with the young David's first steps after leaving the village school the visitor is unable to say. It must, however, be recorded that he entered the postal service at Luton, and for some years journeyed to and from the village in the pursuit of his duties.

"All the time the idea at the back of his mind must have been gathering force, and eventually, as we have already seen, he left the village to pursue his theological studies. His mother supported her son nobly in his determination to devote himself to the higher service, and it must have been a source of great gratification to her when he obtained his L. Th. degree at Durham University in 1909. He was ordained deacon in 1910 and priest in 1911, in which year he relinquished his charge as missionary of the Rond Native Mission, Pretoria, taken up the previous year, for work with the Rustenberg Native Mission. This he left in 1913 to become priest-in-charge of the Krugersdorp Native Mission, and after a year in that position he assumed that of St. Hlamankula Native Missionary in the district of Lourenco Marques, Portuguese East Africa. A period of war service as temporary Chaplain to the Forces brought Mr Trussell overseas in 1917, and after serving in this capacity for two years he returned as priest-in-charge of St. Cyprian Hlamankula, in the diocese of Lebombo.

"The Rev. David Trussell retains affectionate memories of his one-time schoolmistress and regularly corresponds with her. In his last letter, addressed from Zeerust, Transvaal, he states that he has only undertaken work there for a time, and will probably go back to Lebombo. 'The people here', he continues, 'have received me very kindly and cannot do too much to show me the fact. The English and native churches and the Rectory are built on one plot of ground, which is very convenient. Both churches are small, but they are well appointed, while the Rectory is, to me, very sumptuous'."

David Trussell paid a visit to his boyhood haunts in 1920, and preached in the village church. Esther Cundall was not able to go and hear him, for she was a cripple, a circumstance which caused her a great deal of suffering, but never once wiped from her face the smile of welcome the visitor received upon entering her cottage.

The first tractor plough was owned by Bert Facer, of Ward's Farm, and caused such comment as: "Thing like thatun's no bloody good. Carn't plough bloody deep nuff. Nowt like hosses fer that, yew'll see". "Silly ol' bugger wish 'e never 'ad it, yew bet."

It was first used by a rather disgusted farm worker on one of the far fields along Ward's Wood Lane, well out of the way, maybe, of critical eyes!

A horse that liked a pint of good old English ale, as I have already written, Flower by name, was a big black carthorse in the care of Sam Bland. It was a lovely animal with flowing mane and tail. Being Sam's pride and joy, it was daily turned out as if ready for a county show. One day it took a step forward when Dick Bland was holding the leading rein, and placed a great mighty hoof right on his foot. Dick's spontaneous yell of "Get off, get off, yer snotty brute!" caused Flower not the slightest bother.

A man much feared by several generations of choirboys was Matthew Feakes. His flowing beard and large frame were enough in themselves to command respect, but add to them a quick hand with rolled-up newspaper or hymn book and one can see that he was a force to be reckoned with. Matthew was head gardener to Rector Haviland for the thirty-six years that he held this living, and married the Rectory housemaid on the same day that Mr Haviland was married.

An adult member of the church choir, but one who was never heard to sing, was William Davis, under-gardener at the Rectory. After going to an exhibition in London, he was asked by one of Rector Haviland's sons what he liked best. The only thing William could talk about was the wonderful glass which protected the exhibits: "Why, yew coun't even see it!" he remarked. William was a happy man, well content with his lot. When asked if he would like some day to be a head gardener, he replied: "No, I likes tew 'ave me work put tew me."

A man who only drove Rector Haviland from Cambridge to the village in 1868, but who finally remained until the Rector died, was Nathaniel Nottage, coachman. Marrying a local girl, he fathered two boys and two girls, who all at one time or other were in service at the Rectory, the boys as helpers in the stables, and the girls, one as nursemaid and one as parlourmaid. Later, Nathaniel had two nieces who were also in service at the Rectory.

In 1910, the village was honoured by a visit of the East Herts Archaeological Society. The old North Herts Mail reported:

"A party of the above society visited 'Bunyan's Cottage' where the preacher is reputed to have held meetings. At the rear, the party found the village blacksmith, Mr Albert Edward Toyer, busy with hammer and forge. Mr G. Aylott gave an explanatory reading, stating that the building dated from the seventeenth century. Local tradition said it was here Bunyan ministered in the cellar to his hunted flock. The dreamer's feet had oft-times trod the spot where they now stood.

"Mr Aylott referred to the Rev. A.J. Foster's book in which it was suggested that some of the scenes from 'Pilgrim's Progress' were taken from this neighbourhood. Bunyan was 31 when he was arrested near the village for preaching forbidden creeds. The party was much interested when, by Mr Toyer's permission, they peered into the gloomy under-chamber where it is supposed Bunyan's followers secretly worshipped.

"The party then proceeded to the site of the dwelling in which Johann Kellerman had lived nearly a century before. The party inspected the large cellar which remains of the original buildings and saw the furnace which Kellerman used.

"A neighbour entertained the visitors with an account of Kellerman's doings handed down to her by her mother. He was very kind to the village and was approached by all in distress. On one occasion, he heard that a party of gipsies, missing their way in the snow, had fallen into a dell near the turning to the Hoo. Kellerman had them dug out."

Which is a vastly different account of Kellerman's doings from the one generally known. One assumes there was a good reason why he forsook normality to live the life of a recluse.

From 1628-38 William Janeway was Curate of the village church. Two of his sons, both born and baptised in the village, became quite well known. The Janeways belonged to our countryside and the name has not yet disappeared from Hertfordshire. William Janeway was the father of nine other children besides John and James. After completing his ten years at Lilley he became Curate at Ashenden, another Hertfordshire village, the Rector of Ayot St. Lawrence, and afterwards Rector of Kelshall, where, in St. Faith's Church, there is a white marble tablet that bears an inscription telling all that care to look that within this church lie the mortal remains of the Rev. John Janeway, former Fellow of King's College, Cambridge. The tablet relates that John was born October 27, 1633 at Lilley, and that he died during June, 1657, in the twenty-fourth year of his age.

Very early in his life John began to reveal signs of unusual promise as a student. Latin he learned from his father, and afterwards he went to St. Paul's School in London. When he was eleven he could read Hebrew and he acquired skill in mathematics. After having passed an examination with flying colours, he was elected a foundation scholar at Eton, where we read that he was regarded as "the glory of the school". At Oxford, he pursued still further his studies in mathematics and he added to his accomplishments a knowledge of astronomy. He went also to Cambridge, where he was elected a Fellow. After the death of his father, John returned to King's College, where his health was very much impaired by solitary study. He struggled for some time as a private tutor, but became too feeble even for that work, and returned to live with his mother and brother William.

Not for long, however, did he enjoy the peace of rural Hertfordshire. The blight of consumption had overshadowed the Janeways, and seven brothers died before they were forty years of age. Thus in the year 1657 we come to John Janeway entering the "vasty hall of death", and that in June, when the countryside was flooded with the brightest sunshine; when the fields and gardens were full of the scent of roses and of new-mown hay; when the snap-dragons and the sweet williams bloomed before the cottage doors, and the bees were busy among the honeysuckles.

Many are the testimonials to the piety of John from people who knew him, these included the Rev. Marmaduke Tennent, sometime minister of the neighbouring village of Therfield; and the learned Dr. Seth Ward, a native of Ashenden, Bishop of Exeter, and late of Salisbury, with whom John had studied mathematics at Oxford, "looked upon him as one of the wonders of his age, loved him dearly, and could for some time after his death scarce mention his name without tears".

It was agreed that, notwithstanding his many accomplishments, John was without conceit or affectation and with no trace of selfishness. "His deportment was sweet and lovely, his demeanour courteous and obliging." A saint, indeed!

John's more famous brother, James, was born in 1636 during the reign of Charles I, the fourth son of William. When he was about nineteen, he went as a student to Christ Church, Oxford, where he graduated as a Bachelor of Arts, but when Charles II was invited to occupy the throne that had been wrested from his father, James left Oxford to serve as a tutor to George Stringer at Windsor, and during the Great Plague of 1665 he went to London as a non-conformist preacher at a time when several conventicles were being opened. Relieved by the Declaration of Indulgence of 1672 the friends of Janeway built for him a meeting house in Jamaica Row, Rotherhithe, in which his preaching attracted large congregations.

Not for long, however, was James allowed to preach in peace. When Charles II favoured the Declaration of Indulgence his aim had been to relieve the Catholics from persecution, and this so enraged Members of the House of Commons, the supporters of the Church of England and other Protestants, that there seemed to be a danger that Charles would be deposed. This was a peril that the King was particularly anxious to avoid, because during the period that he had been excluded from the throne and from England he had spent three years in Paris in poverty, wearing patched shirts and cobbled boots, depending upon the charity of others and eating his meals in taverns. Now, not even to serve the Catholics, would he abandon the comforts of Whitehall. Thus he bent to the storm, and in 1673 the freedom that had been bestowed was withdrawn, and James Janeway's meeting house was wrecked by soldiers.

Undismayed, his friends built for him another and a larger place of worship, and his popularity aroused so much enmity among his opponents that he was in danger of not only imprisonment but also assassination. While he was walking one day along the side of the river a shot was fired at him, missing him by only inches. On another day, soldiers entered his conventicle shouting: "Down with him!" Some soldiers climbed upon a bench that they might drag him from his pulpit, but the bench gave way and James escaped, his friends disguising him with a coloured coat and a white hat.

Like his brothers, James was haunted by the family spectre of consumption and eventually surrendered to it on March 16, 1674, but his memory was to live for a very long time yet, for he had written books that continued to be printed and read at least until 1863. The most well-known of his books was published in 1671, bearing the massive title: "Token for Children: Being An Exact Account Of The Conversion, Holy and Exemplary Lives, and Joyful Deaths Of Several Young Children. To Which Is Now Added, Prayers And Graces, Fitted For The Use By Little Children. By James Janeway, Minister of the Gospel." The book was printed in London "by W.O. for T. Norris, at the Looking-glass; and A. Bettesworth, at the Red Lion, both on London-bridge".

So ended the lives of two sons of the village, who each in his own way, and beset by many difficulties, fought the good fight to the end.

Chapter 17

A Boy's War

Written by Arthur Bland with additions by the Author

During the Second World War, life in the village was a mixture of modernity and feudalism. The Squirearchy, prevalent for centuries, was non-existent and the best of feudalism came back into our lives. Everyone gave their services willingly to help in the cause of food production. Farming folk and factory workers were all one people. All loved and respected the countryside. Villagers gleaned the fields for corn for their fowls which then inhabited nearly every garden.

This was the age of the "Dig for Victory" campaign, and dig they did. Many gardens were regularly manured from the little wooden, spider-ridden privy beside the garden path, and the cabbages grew, the potatoes yielded, the peas became swollen. Farm horses still pulled carts; the self-binder was still an important piece of machinery, and potato "riddling" was done in the farmyard. Peace reigned in the fields; rabbits roamed at will; boys went birds-nesting and climbed trees; girls played ball against brick walls; real old characters still sat in a corner of the Silver Lion. The Home Guard exercised in the fields; the Auxiliary Fire Service extinguished imaginary fires at the "Topend"; the Special Constabulary patrolled nearly every evening, and Charlie Toyer owned the Post Office and general stores.

He managed to cope with all the worries of ration cards and coupons on top of the complexities of the Post Office. If that were not enough, he and his wife Ivy looked after two evacuees, in addition to their own two children, as indeed many other people did, too. Charlie had an assistant, that very good-hearted person "Joyce". No man could cower her; she would soon "fix" the children if they were cheeky, and was mainly responsible for the organisation of food supplies stored in the Rectory, ready for use if the need arose.

Mr and Mrs Fred Webb ran "The Stores". Always generous to the children, Mrs Webb often included a few extra sweets in their bags. Fred was indispensible to many villagers in that he recharged accumulators for their radio sets.

Unfortunately, for a time his good lady became the victim of a "racket". It had been the habit for customers to place empty soft drink bottles in a line on the floor just inside the door. Some children discovered that by taking one empty bottle back and craftily picking several off the floor, they could obtain enough refund to buy another bottle of drink. The word soon got around, but the system developed to such an extent that discovery was inevitable!

Ada Lawrence kept the remaining general shop. To many children that shop was the most interesting, possibly because of the heavy shade from a magnificent horse chestnut tree which grew opposite, and the high counter which gave the shop a mysterious atmosphere — or was it the cat that always seemed to be asleep in the window?

The butcher's shop next door was managed by Dan Poulter, who kept the shop spotlessly clean and served his customers well. Travelling from Luton every day meant an early start for Dan, who was known for his perennial comment: "It was cold in Wardown Lake at six o'clock this morning!"

The village's two inns were a source of social life to many people. All the trials and tribulations of war could be aired by the populance in these homely establishments. They also provided the essential release of tensions for those who, on occasion, found their cross too much to bear.

Has there ever been a parrot to equal the one kept at the inn on the village Green? That amazing bird, an African Grey, could not only swear like a trooper, but was capable of barking like its owners' dog, whistling the dog, calling its owners to the bar and so on. It would have made a perfect bar tender had it been able to serve drinks!

While the pubs provided good cheer, the milk for our daily "cuppa" was provided mainly by two farms, Ward's Farm run by the Clarke family and Church Farm run by the Elliott family. Both farms supplied good rich milk from the churn.

Church Farm is possibly the only one that really lived up to the "story book" image; perhaps because it had a large garden which was well kept. The apple trees were there, so were the ducks and the pond. There once stood in the rickyard an ancient tractor and a very old car. The remains of a Hertfordshire Waggon, built by village men, gracefully passed away in one of the meadows of Church Farm. All of these things helped to create a place of interest to the wartime youngsters, but above all, the Elliott family made it a place of lasting memories by their actions. It was not uncommon for a dozen or so children to be allowed to play games in and around the "mysterious" farm buildings, and for many years they have played in "Elliotts' Meadows" and never have they been ejected.

The village boasted businesses during the war which would still be beneficial today. "Lennie" Lawrence owned a coal delivery business. He was small of stature, yet must have been very strong, for he managed to hump sacks of coal on to his flat waggon, drawn by, at one time, a large "grey" horse, with an ease that would have shamed a larger man. In his seventies, he pushed a hand cart loaded with garden produce to Hitchin, a distance of about six miles, and in his eighties still rode a bicycle. "Lennie" also made straw hives. Once a bee-keeper himself, he was well aware of the preference of bees, as were many good apiarists, who preferred in recent years to purchase "Lennie's" straw hives rather than rely on modern fabricated ones.

Frank Webb owned a shoe-mending shop attached to a lovely old cottage — which has since been modernised — set in a charming olde-worlde garden. His workshop was always a source of interest with its rows of boots and shoes set neatly on shelves; its treadle sewing machine, brads and awls; its tins of boot polish and leather preservative for sale; its cast-iron "feet", and pervading all the satisfying aroma of new leather. Frank was an expert at his job and took great pride in his work. Having lost a leg in the First World War, he could not easily get about. However, by using a specially adapted bicycle with one stationary pedal and the other for propelling, he managed to travel quite long distances in the course of his work.

Unlike today, in those years of stress, when labour was at a premium for war work, the village had a road sweeper. George Bishop, a Lengthman, not only swept the road, he also kept the verges tidy and the ditches clear. These latter, perhaps now a figure of fun, were not the invention of village idiots. They served a very useful purpose in dispersing rain water very quickly. Today, there are no ditches, but just take a look at the water that stands in the roadside after a heavy shower!

Bob Titmuss was the village Sexton and was a woodcutter in his daily employment. Bob was one of the few who remained a real countryman until his death some years ago. He chose to ignore the rat-race and spent his life nurturing the woodlands. He witnessed the gaunt, bare branches of the winter trees; he saw with delight the bursting buds of spring, and sheltered beneath the greenery on a hot summer's day; he discovered the new nests, the warm eggs, the bare, ugly young birds, and watched them eventually fly away, free and happy. A wise man, indeed!

Many a lad would have his hair cut, short back and sides, either by Perce Eddy or Bob Earle, suffering the tortures of hand clippers in order to appear smart at a village social function.

Bob Earle was also a "wart charmer". He used a beefsteak and magical utterings to make the warts disappear, and it really did work. By what means remains a mystery to this day.

While callow youth and mature adult enjoyed the entertainment of a social evening, the children looked forward to their own special event, the annual children's party. As the party was usually held in January, a fall of snow often added to the pleasure of walking up the bottom Rectory drive to "The Rectory Room", which at one time was a schoolroom for the Haviland children. On either side of the drive the conifers, heavily laden with snow, their sweet tangy aroma mingling with that of damp earth and burning wood, imparted a sense of an unreal Christmas card scene, as if one was not really there, but was looking on from some isolated spot at oneself plodding happily through the snow, amid the peace of nature's winter.

It is worth having another look at the bottom Rectory drive. In late winter there appeared a mass of snowdrops, the largest concentrated mass to be seen. As the snowdrops reached perfection, aconites began to appear, turning the white carpet into a yellow foretaste of sunny days to come. About halfway along the drive grew the tallest fir tree for many a mile. Partially hidden by dense yew trees, the remains of the old Parsonage House stood like a gaunt sentinel, a reminder of past glories and a life now gone, gradually being eaten away by the elements.

After the war, the children's party was held in the Victory Hall. This much-maligned building, a 1914-18 war hut, bought by the village, was worthy of preservation. Serving as a village hall on the present site of the Cassel Hall, it survived the flappers of the 'twenties, the depression of the 'thirties — when it may well have been "pinched" for firewood — Army boots of the 'forties, square dancing of the 'fifties and "pop" groups of the 'sixties. Ugly it may have been, but the Victory Hall was a nostalgic reminder of the "good old days" when entertainment was self-made. Alas, it is no more.

The entertainment field cannot be left without mention of the wartime film shows so generously provided by the late John Gibbs. It is rather ironical that the films he showed — starring Tom Walls, Will Hay, Moore Mariott and suchlike — were more up to date then than many of those shown today on television!

It was not uncommon in the early war years for hundreds of troops to take over the meadows and woods. Convoys of vehicles regularly passed through the village, sometimes in a continuous stream for many hours on end. This activity caused much excitement among the children, and likewise the soldiers were usually happy to chat with the children. On one occasion, some soldiers cheerfully rid themselves of extra weight by giving practice bullets to the children. These contained toy caps fired by a percussion cap. Much fun was had by placing the point of a nail on the percussion cap and duly clouting it with a hammer to obtain an explosion. Another cheerful hand-out by the soldiers were iron-ration biscuits. How they laughed to see the children desperately trying to bite through the steel-like food!

In addition to soldiers, the Fleet Air Arm was prominent in the sky above the village, pilots being trained at Luton Airport. At times the sky was dotted with dozens of yellow-painted Tiger Moth and Magister aircraft, all individually performing aerobatics. The village can perhaps claim to have helped the success of the war in the air by being honoured with the presence of the prototype Auster aircraft flown from a meadow adjacent to the A505.

Such an aircraft would have been useful to the villagers when they discovered that almost overnight the War Department had taken over the Hoo and denied access to the public. At first indignant that the common — which for many years had given them so much pleasure in the form of picnics, games of cricket and so on — had been taken from them, the villagers soon became resigned to the fact that it was all in a good cause. But they did not realise that this was virtually the end of the Hoo as a very pleasant and beautiful heath.

About this time, the village had a great character in the form of Hattle Champkin, known to all as "Tat". His singing in the pubs was a "sight to hear". Many times the children would press their faces against the outside of a window of his favourite pub to watch "Tat" performing. Loved by all, he was tall and upright and would invariably be seen smoking a clay pipe with its bowl facing earthwards. Another character was a great drinker. Often on leaving the pub, too drunk to stand, he was helped aboard his bicycle, given a push and would then cycle home as if he was completely sober — providing, that is, that no one got in his way!

If the village characters gave us entertainment so, too, did the organisers of the village fete. This annual event was of necessity abandoned during most of the war years but was revived again just before, or just after, the end of hostilities and was held in the Rectory grounds, as tradition had dictated for many years.

The beautifully kept lawns of the Rectory grounds formed an idyllic setting for the fete, while the palatial Victorian mansion — now unhappily demolished — gave one a sense of "belonging". This was "home" to all villagers, be they pub-goers, church-goers, agnostic or atheist. Those were halcyon days when farmers, landowners and villagers were all one community. Of course, there were grumbles and grouses, but all knew they were part of a family — a community — in which goodwill predominated.

The Church Commissioners were perhaps unwittingly responsible for inaugurating the beginning of the end of the village as a true community. It would appear to an outsider looking on that that body has of necessity to concern itself more with finance than Christianity. After some years of dithering they concluded that the huge Rectory was uneconomic and sold it, deciding after many stormy meetings between diocese and villagers, that a resident Rector was a financial burden it could no longer tolerate. It seems strange that in those early post-war years, when empty houses were like gold-dust, the powers that be could not have had converted the whole of the Rectory to flats for young or elderly villagers. A few of its many rooms had already been converted before the last resident Rector left and let to "outsiders". Some young village couples about to be married, including regular worshippers, applied to rent these flats. Only one couple was successful. The grounds, once the pride of Matthew Feakes and which would have pleased the expert eye of Capability Brown, were left unkempt for a time, then subsequently sold together with planning permission for building plots.

It is worthwhile reflecting on the fact that this Chiltern village as we know it today was largely designed in the eighteenth century by the Georgians, and a very good job they made of it, too. Take away the modern houses, Georgian dwellings or Georgianised cottages, and only a handful of properties would be left, so great was the change in that period. Remove the straight hedges planted by the Georgians and most of the woodlands, which did not exist prior to that time, and the village can be visualised as a very different place from now, a community dominated by the strip method of farming with vast open tracts of land to east and west.

Until the middle nineteen-thirties the village, topographically at least, had hardly changed since the Georgian period, although a few Victorian houses had been built. With the advent of the Second World War a few houses only were added and during that period the natural environment was preserved much more so than today. Although Great Britain was at war, paradoxically the countryside around here was for most of the time completely peaceful and quiet.

Hedges bordered nearly every field and were well kept, although labour was short and few mechanical aids were available. Every lane had a wealth of wild flowers, shrubs and trees, each giving colour according to their season. Beautiful crab apple trees, many in their variety; sloes, hazels, even the occasional cherry, gooseberry and raspberry, provided a ready feast for all. Wild strawberries abounded on the land between the Hoo and Pegsdon Hills. There, a properly constructed dew pond, set among the scrub, provided a meeting place for the things of nature. This dew pond — and another — have been restored by the Lilley Society.

A similar patch of scrubland, relic of the pre-Enclosure open land, then existed on the west side of Lilley Wood. Sheltered from the easterly winds, yet open to the sun, it was a natural haven, full of interest. Many different flowers grew there, and a fallen tree, bereft of branches and slowly rotting, was many things to many children — sometimes a pirate ship, sometimes a Churchill tank, but more often than not the scene of "mothers and fathers". In late summer the air was richly scented with marjoram; dewberries, a fruit related to the blackberry but far superior in flavour, grew in abundance. Mignonette, ladies' bed-straw, yarrow and various varieties of campanula were among the flowers visited by the butterflies which frequented the area, and indeed, still do.

These were times when the wide use of pesticides and herbicides had not begun. Birds such as the spotted flycatcher, sparrow hawk and red-backed shrike, though not common, could often be seen.

Shortly after the war, a Montague's Harrier nested in the scrub near Pegsdon Hills. This bird was rare in the area and unfortunately two village lads (the writers of this chapter, in fact) found its nest by accident. They took two of the four eggs and later some Hexton lads took the remaining two. The pair of Harriers never returned. Other birds, white throats, chiff chaffs and various varieties of warblers were then common. Now that their habitat has been destroyed they are rarely seen outside of the woods.

Modern farm machinery has enabled the farmer to use his land to the full, albeit that its innovation has inevitably caused the loss of the much-loved areas of scrubland. Had they been available during the war, combine harvesters and grain-drying plants would have saved one particular crop which was lost through freak weather. That year, the corn had been cut and shocked (or stooked) when the weather suddenly turned cold. A heavy snow storm covered the tops of the shocks with about two inches of snow. The resulting heat and moisture caused the grain to germinate and fresh green growth topped each shock of corn in a matter of days.

In retrospect, people are inclined to say that the weather was kinder in the "old days". This does seem so, but one suspects the main reason for such thoughts is that the working day was longer, often starting at 6 am on the farms. During the war, double summertime ensured daylight until 11.30 pm in the summer months. During one school summer holiday it rained nearly every day for the whole six weeks!

A particularly interesting winter occurred in 1942 or 1943. Hard frost had solidified the ground. This was followed by a very heavy fall of snow, but within a few hours the temperature soared and the snow melted rapidly. The resultant water was unable to soak into the frosted ground and large lakes were formed. Almost immediately the temperature fell again and hard frost turned the lakes into skating rinks. The two largest were in the area stretching across the meadow to Doozley Pond, which was itself overflowing across the road, and in the valley area of Stocking Hill Field. These lakes made for excellent safe skating as the overlying frozen water was only a few inches deep.

Doozley Pond was, until the demise of the steam traction engine, a relatively clean pond. "Ollie" Saville often stopped his engine at Doozley to take on water on his journey from Wandon End to the farms at threshing time. Boys would crowd around the traction engine keen to watch its working, just as the village boys, then grown up and fighting for their country, had done when they were children.

Perhaps the village men and women serving in the Armed Forces remembered "Ollie" when their thoughts turned to home. They were certainly in the thoughts of the villagers, and those who did not return are remembered for ever, and rightly so, but are those who did return remembered so well?

Whether we remember or not, the men and women from every city, town, village and hamlet in Britain did not fight the Second World War in vain. They preserved for us its rich traditions, its children, a country which still allows the individual the greatest freedom in the world.

How much that freedom was appreciated on VE night in 1945 is now difficult to imagine. The village celebrated with a huge bonfire on the Green. Every house wore bunting or a Union Jack. People were intoxicated with happiness. Villagers gathered in the evening around the bonfire, drank each other's health in beer from the pub on the Green and danced and sang with joy, accompanied by Charlie Read on his cornet.

And the parrot sat on his perch thinking: "It's great to be alive!"

Books Published by THE BOOK CASTLE

CHANGES IN OUR LANDSCAPE: ASPECTS OF BEDFORDSHIRE, BUCKINGHAMSHIRE and the CHILTERNS, 1947–1992: from the photographic work of Eric Meadows. 350+ fascinating colour and monochrome pictures by the area's leading landscape photographer. Detailed introduction and captions.

JOURNEYS INTO HERTFORDSHIRE: Anthony Mackay. Foreword by The Marquess of Salisbury, Hatfield House, Nearly 200 superbly detailed ink drawings depict the towns, buildings and landscape of this still predominantly rural county.

JOURNEYS INTO BEDFORDSHIRE: Anthony Mackay. Foreword by The Marquess of Tavistock, Woburn Abbey. A lavish book of over 150 evocative ink drawings.

NORTH CHILTERNS CAMERA, 1863–1954: FROM THE THURSTON COLLECTION IN LUTON MUSEUM: edited by Stephen Bunker. Rural landscapes, town views, studio pictures and unique royal portraits by the area's leading early photographer.

LEAFING THROUGH LITERATURE: WRITERS' LIVES IN HERTFORDSHIRE AND BEDFORDSHIRE: David Carroll. Illustrated short biographies of many famous authors and their connections with these counties.

THROUGH VISITORS' EYES: A BEDFORDSHIRE ANTHOLOGY: edited by Simon Houfe. Impressions of the county by famous visitors over the last four centuries, thematically arranged and illustrated with line drawings.

THE HILL OF THE MARTYR: AN ARCHITECTURAL HISTORY OF ST. ALBANS ABBEY: Eileen Roberts. Scholarly and readable chronological narrative history of Hertfordshire and Bedfordshire's famous cathedral. Fully illustrated with photographs and plans.

LOCAL WALKS: SOUTH BEDFORDSHIRE and NORTH CHILTERNS: Vaughan Basham. Twenty-seven thematic circular walks.

CHILTERN WALKS: HERTFORDSHIRE, BEDFORDSHIRE and NORTH BUCKINGHAMSHIRE: Nick Moon. Completes the trilogy of circular walks, in association with the Chiltern Society.

CHILTERN WALKS: BUCKINGHAMSHIRE: Nick Moon. In association with the Chiltern Society, one of a series of three guides to the whole Chilterns. Thirty circular walks.

CHILTERN WALKS: OXFORDSHIRE and WEST BUCKINGHAMSHIRE: Nick Moon. In association with the Chiltern Society, another book of thirty circular walks.

ECHOES: TALES and LEGENDS of BEDFORDHSIRE and HERTFORDSHIRE: Vic Lea. Thirty, compulsively retold historical incidents.

COUNTRY AIR: SUMMER and AUTUMN: Ron Wilson. The Radio Northampton presenter looks month by month at the countryside's wildlife, customs and lore.

COUNTRY AIR: WINTER and SPRING: Ron Wilson. This companion volume completes the year in the countryside.

WHIPSNADE WILD ANIMAL PARK: 'MY AFRICA': Lucy Pendar. Foreword by Andrew Forbes. Introduction by Gerald Durrell. Inside story of sixty years of the Park's animals and people – full of anecdotes, photographs and drawings.

FARM OF MY CHILDHOOD, 1925–1947: Mary Roberts. An almost vanished lifestyle on a remote farm near Flitwick.

SWANS IN MY KITCHEN: The Story of a Swan Sanctuary: Lis Dorer. Foreword by Dr Philip Burton. Tales of her dedication to the survival of these beautiful birds through her sanctuary near Hemel Hempstead.

A LASTING IMPRESSION: Michael Dundrow. An East End boy's wartime experiences as an evacuee on a Chilterns farm at Totternhoe.

EVA'S STORY: CHESHAM SINCE the TURN of the CENTURY: Eva Rance. The ever-changing twentieth-century, especially the early years at her parents' general stores, Tebby's, in the High Street.

DUNSTABLE DECADE: THE EIGHTIES: – A Collection of Photographs: Pat Lovering. A souvenir book of nearly 300 pictures of people and events in the 1980s.

DUNSTABLE IN DETAIL: Nigel Benson. A hundred of the town's buildings and features, plus town trail map.

OLD DUNSTABLE: Bill Twaddle. A new edition of this collection of early photographs.

BOURNE AND BRED: A DUNSTABLE BOYHOOD BETWEEN THE WARS: Colin Bourne. An elegantly written, well-illustrated book capturing the spirit of the town over fifty years ago.

ROYAL HOUGHTON: Pat Lovering. Illustrated history of Houghton Regis from the earliest times to the present.

MURDERS and MYSTERIES, PEOPLE and PLOTS: A Buckinghamshire, Bedfordshire and Northamptonshire Miscellany: John Houghton. This fascinating book of true tales roams around three counties and covers three centuries.

THE CHANGING FACE OF LUTON: An Illustrated History: Stephen Bunker, Robin Holgate and Marian Nichols. Luton's development from earliest times to the present busy industrial town. Illustrated in colour and monochrome. The three authors from Luton Museum are all experts in local history, archaeology, crafts and social history.

BETWEEN THE HILLS: The Story of Lilley, a Chiltern Village: Roy Pinnock. A priceless piece of our heritage – the rural beauty remains but the customs and way of life described here have largely disappeared.

THE MEN WHO WORE STRAW HELMETS: POLICING LUTON, 1840–1974: Tom Madigan. Meticulously chronicled history; dozens of rare photographs; author served Luton Police for nearly fifty years.

THE TALL HITCHIN SERGEANT: A Victorian Crime Novel based on fact: Edgar Newman. Mixes real police officers and authentic background with an exciting storyline.

Specially for Children

ADVENTURE ON THE KNOLLS: A STORY OF IRON AGE BRITAIN: Michael Dundrow. Excitement on Totternhoe Knolls as ten-year-old John finds himself back in those dangerous times, confronting Julius Caesar and his army.

THE RAVENS: ONE BOY AGAINST THE MIGHT OF ROME: James Dyer. On the Barton hills and in the south-east of England as the men of the great fort of Ravensburgh (near Hexton) confront the invaders.